T0158523

Interrupted Lives:

Four Women's Stories of Internment During World War II in the Philippines

THIS BOOK IS DEDICATED TO THE THOUSANDS OF PEOPLE WHO LIVED THROUGH INTERNMENT BY THE JAPANESE IN THE PHILIPPINE CAMPS DURING WORLD WAR II, ESPECIALLY THE WOMEN AND CHILDREN.

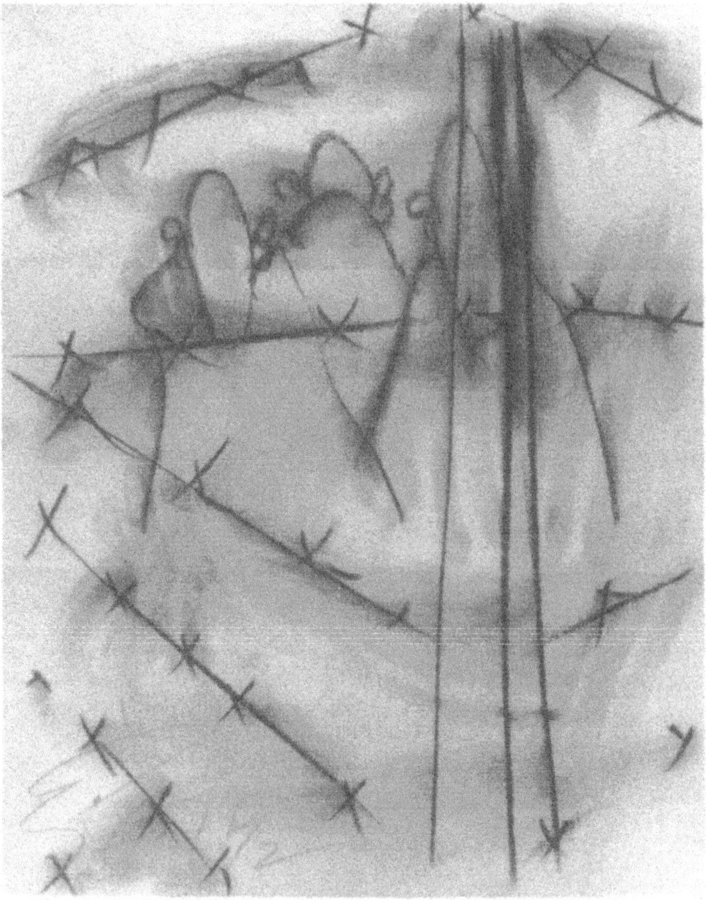

This is What Happens..., #II, by E.J. Gold,
charcoal on Sennelier Pastel paper, $12^{3}/4$" x 16", 1992.

Interrupted Lives:

Four Women's Stories of Internment During World War II in the Philippines

Margaret Sams

Sascha Jean Jansen

Jane S. Wills

Karen Kerns Lewis

with an introduction by

Lily Nova

edited by

Lily Nova and Iven Lourie

Artemis Books

Penn Valley, California

3rd printing 2018, printed in the U.S.A,.
ISBN: 978-0-9645181-9-3
Cover design by Gailyn Porter
Cover art, frontispiece and chapter art by E.J. Gold
[from the series *This is What Happens…* charcoal on Sennelier paper, 12 ¼' X 16'm 1992, © 1995 Heidelberg Editions International]

The editors wish to thank: The University of Wisconsin Press for permission to use an excerpt from *Forbidden Family: A Wartime Memoir*, by Margaret Sams, published in 1989; Madeline (Gigi) Poston, whose sketches from Santo Tomas appear on pages 30 and 109; the late Jerry Sams, who let us include some of the secret photographs he took at Santo Tomas during his internment; and the late Jack Eisen for his newspaper research and archive headlines. Lily Nova thanks her mother, Adelaide W. Kintz, for her inspiration.

This edition is also dedicated to these contributors who have passed—they enriched our lives immeasurably:

Margaret Sams	**1916 - 2011**	
Jane S. Wills	**1917 - 2007**	**(??not certain)**
Lily Nova	**1933 - 2016**	
Sascha Jean Jansen	**1936 - 2018**	

Table of Contents

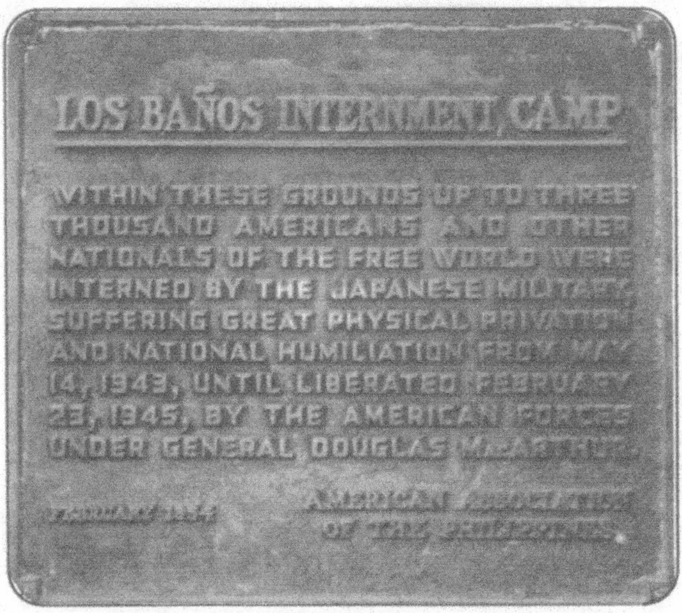

Plaque at Los Baños honoring the Internees, 1943 - 1945

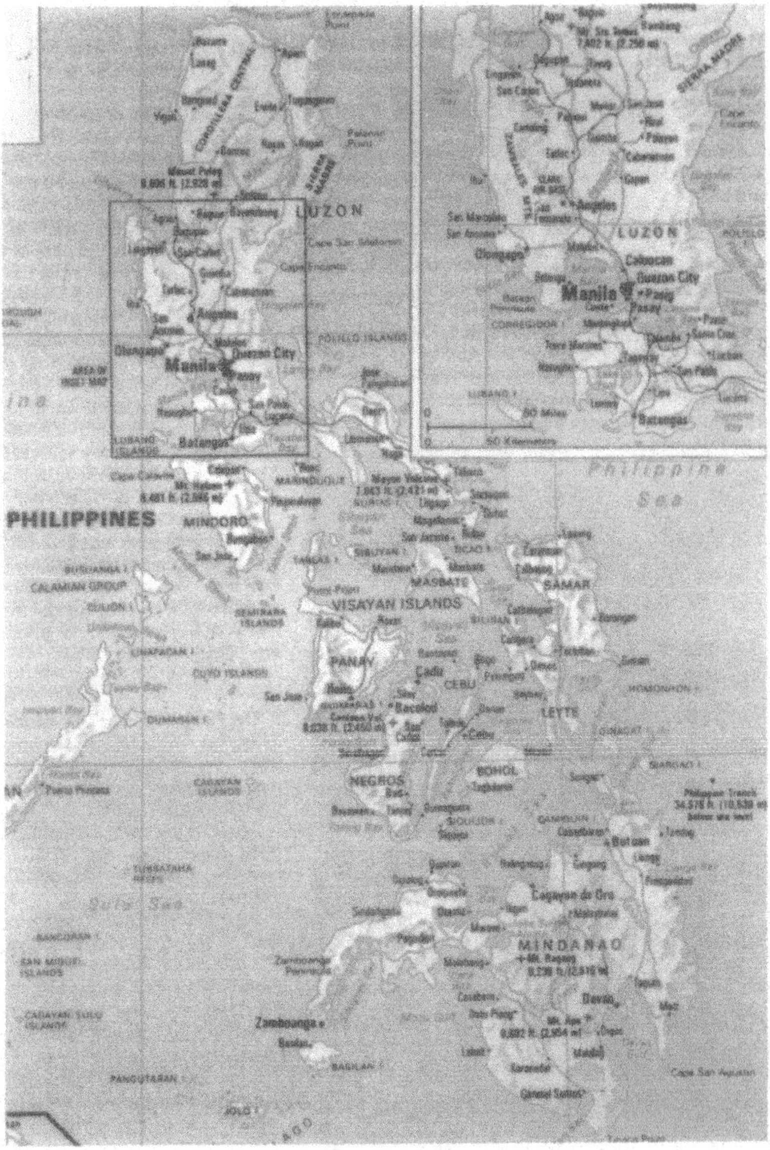

Map of the Philippines

INTRODUCTION

When the war started, I was a child of eight and my parents had just put my sister and me in a Catholic convent near Los Angeles, California. They were separating—my father was employed at a defense plant and my mother had just joined the U.S.O. and moved to King City in northern California. I didn't know much about the war except that people talked of it and lots of Uncle Sam pictures appeared on billboards and the radio broadcast reports of battles. I just knew that my life was changing drastically and I didn't like it at all.

We had never been in a Catholic church before. My mother had sent us to Presbyterian Sunday School and my father was opposed to any organized religion. The choice was made, however, to send us to the convent since it seemed to be the best one of a short list of boarding schools we could afford. We were very poor during the Depression and Dad's work at the defense plant was his first steady employment in years.

My sister and I tried to survive the dark atmosphere and strict discipline at the convent and dreamt of the day we would be set free. I hated it there and waited all week for Dad's visit on Saturday. Fortunately we were "liberated" by a visitation of chicken pox. (Maybe we are the only kids who were happy to get the disease.) By the time the school authorities learned what those little spots were on my arms and back we had contaminated the whole place and were delighted when we were sent home, never to return.

My dad packed us into the back of his Model A

Ford, on a stormy, dark night with lightning flashing and thunder roaring above, and drove us to King City to plead with Mother to come home to her family. As I remember it, he burst into the U.S.O. Center and found her serving coffee and doughnuts to the soldiers and announced that she must come home to her husband and children.

She did come home to us but decided not to include my dad and we moved to Westwood where she started training as a draftsperson for MacDonald-Douglas Aircraft Co.

When Pearl Harbor was being bombed, my uncle Harry was an officer in the U.S. Navy on a submarine in the South Pacific. His wife, Kitty, and new baby were in the civilian housing adjoining the Pearl Harbor base and my grandmother had just arrived from the States to visit them the night before. They were expecting Harry to return soon. Grandma was up early and listening to the radio. She had heard planes and loud noises but was not sure what was happening. The radio announcer said that Pearl Harbor on the island of Oahu had just been attacked by the Japanese. She went to awaken Kitty to find out where Oahu was and in a minute learned that the attack was happening less than three miles away. Now they listened with horror to the sounds of the bombs and saw flames leaping from some buildings a few blocks away.

In 1942 we received word that Uncle Harry's sub, the U.S.S. Trout, did not return from a dangerous mission in Asia and we hoped that he would survive somehow. Grandma and Kitty went on helping in the war effort and holding onto the thought that he might be a prisoner somewhere.

On the homefront, I was aware of the progress of the war with radio reports, Roosevelt's *Fireside Chats* and movie house *News of the World* footage. The beach areas of Los Angeles where the aircraft companies were located were dotted with *barrage balloons* to fool enemy aircraft and I could see a number of these from my house. Rationing on many important foods and gasoline was a big part of our life during the war. There were shortages of many products including fabric and we collected newspapers to help the war effort.

In 1952, as a student at U.C.L.A., I met Karen Kerns. She was more than a year ahead of me and an art major. We roomed together for a semester and became fast friends. I knew that she had been in the Philippines during the war but she didn't talk about it much and somehow I didn't question her about it. I guess I was pretty involved in my own preoccupations with school and a marriage that had ended in annulment. Karen was the kind of person that made me feel comfortable and relaxed—it seems we were friends from the start.

In 1990 I got the idea of putting together a book of stories from women who had something to say about their experiences during World War II. My mother was retired and writing her own memoirs of her 35 years as a Recreation Director for the Red Cross all over the world. I began working with an editor friend, Iven Lourie, and together we collected narratives, letters, poems, and interviews from many women. I contacted Karen and told her of my project. She promised to send me her manuscript telling of her experiences in Santo Tomas as an internee which she had been wanting to complete for a number of years. Karen also put me in touch with her friend, Sascha Jean Weinzheimer Jansen, who lived in the Philippines as a child. I talked to Sascha, now living in Hawaii, and she sent me part of her screenplay, a dramatization of what happened to her and her family at the start of the war, and let me interview her over the phone. The interview and a portion of her screenplay are included in this publication.

One of the books I found in my search for women's experiences during World War II was *Forbidden Family*, a powerful and very personal account written by Margaret Sams about her war years in Santo Tomas and Los Baños internment camps. Her poignant and often gripping story touched my heart and I was thrilled when I saw on the dust jacket that she lived only a few miles from me. I wrote her a letter and got to see her soon after that. She is a warm and generous person and was kind enough to let me interview her—asking her to relive this very painful time in her life.

In preparing this book (the longer manuscript is nearly complete and we are still seeking a publisher), Iven and I wanted to put together the four stories that came to us about life in the Santo Tomas and Los Baños camps during the war and make it available to those attending the Reunions commemorating the Fifty Year Anniversary of the Liberation of those camps. Each story has its own perspective and view of what happened there. Each person who lived through it has his/her own incredible story of the daily trials, difficulties, sacrifices and small joys. What we offer here is only a tiny glimpse of the immense picture of how people were affected by the war, how the upheaval caught them and how they dealt with it. Two of these stories are from a child's perspective, two are from mothers.

There are many books available on the intense, often harrowing, sometimes terrible experiences during World War II. Lives were lost, twisted, turned around and dramatically changed. In offering this book, our aim is to awaken a spark of understanding for our common heritage. This war affected all of us and we inherited the world that was left when it ended.

Lily Nova, January 1995

FINAL MORNING EXTRA

San Francisco Chronicle

The City's Only Home-Owned Newspaper

U.S. AT WAR!

PARATROOPS LAND IN PHILIPPINES!

America at War!

EDITORIAL

Japs Bomb Hawaii, Invade Thailand

350 Slain—Then Tokyo Declares War on U. S., Britain; President Roosevelt Will Go Before Congress Today!

Pacific Coast Springs to Wartime Alert; Leaves Are Canceled, Guns Manned

FDR on Air

Raids Took a Heavy Toll,

Raiders Fly From Hidden Aircraft Carrier; Guam Is 'Surrounded'; Wake Falls

NEW YORK, Dec. 8 (AP) — Royal Arch Gunnison, broadcasting to WOR-Mutual from Manila, reported today that Japanese parachute troops had been landed in the Philippines.

San Francisco Chronicle, Dec. 8, 1941

Santo Tomas University

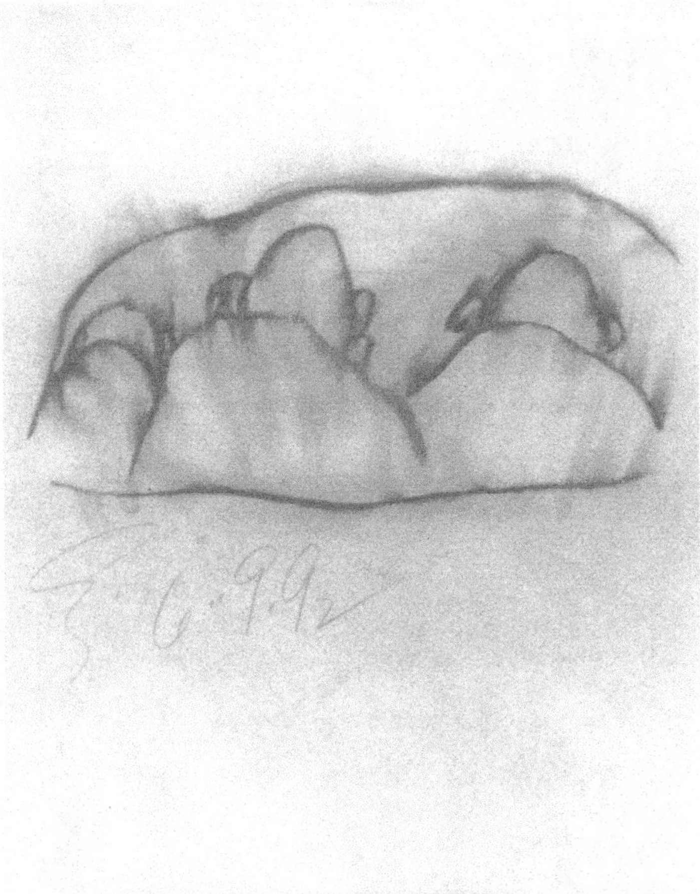

This is What Happens..., #III, by E.J. Gold,
charcoal on Sennelier Pastel paper, 12 3/4" x 16", 1992.

Margaret & Jerry Sams with David & Gerry Ann in 1945

Margaret & Jerry in 1994

Margaret Sams

Margaret Sams was born in Oklahoma and brought up in Beaumont, California. In 1936 she journeyed to the Philippines to marry Bob Sherk, a fellow student who had gone before her to work as a supervisor in the gold mines north of Baguio, about a day's trip from Manila. When World War II broke out Bob was captured, survived the Bataan Death March but died as a Japanese prisoner. Margaret, then twenty-five, and their son David, then four, were first interned in the Santo Tomas camp in Manila from January 1942 until March 1944, and then in the Los Baños camp until their liberation in February 1945. While in Santo Tomas Margaret met and married Jerry Sams.

Margaret's story of how an ordinary young woman met the challenges of extraordinarily difficult circumstances is told in her book, Forbidden Family. "It was written the hard way," she said. "Five days a week I took our son to nursery school for two hours. I sat in the back seat of the car, with my typewriter on my knees, while I waited for him—and remembered, and remembered...." Once written, it was put in a drawer and forgotten for more than thirty years. Friends eventually prevailed upon her to publish her story and make it available to others.

We are including photographs taken illegally by the daring Jerry Sams during their internment using a forbidden camera. The following is from an interview with Margaret Sams at her home in Chicago Park, California.

The Liberation:

We knew something was happening outside our walls because we could hear airplanes in the distance and sometimes we heard artillery fire in the direction of Manila. A few airplanes flew right over us but we'd been ordered by the Japanese not to look up under penalty of death (I couldn't understand why, but I didn't want to get shot) so most of us kept our heads down. Jerry built a radio (strictly forbidden) to which we listened every night. The Japanese abandoned the camp for a week in January (they got scared when they heard the U.S. Army had landed nearby) but they came back the following week.

"We hadn't been asleep long this time when our good friend Doc burst in...'For Christ's sake, get up. They're gone!' I couldn't believe it, and yet I could hear people racing up and down the hall, lights were beginning to come on, fires were being lit in cook shanties. *Something* had happened, certainly. Jerry just lay in bed and said 'Hell, you've all gone stir crazy. Go back to bed and let me sleep.' Nothing we could say or do would make him get up and look around. Doc went away then and in a few minutes the fellow...at the end cubicle arrived from the bachelor barracks. Immediately he started pounding on the wall, and in a minute put his head over the partition and said, 'You rembember what I promised? I said when the Japs left I'd open my last cans and we'd have a real chow.' With that Nadia and he came over with coffee, canned milk, and Spam....With the coming of the coffee Jerry got up. We had no more than gotten the water hot when Doc burst in again and said,

'Jerry, your time has come to rise and shine. For God's sake, break out your receiver and let's see what's going on.' My first thought upon hearing that the Japanese were gone had been the sugar under our own bed, some people's first thoughts had been looting the Japanese barracks. Then came the news (they *were* gone!).

"How can I ever hope to picture the wild excitement of that dawn? Our neighbors were dumbfounded when we produced the radio, and I was amazed that we really had been able to keep it a secret, for there were times when I had been sure they had looked at us askance. Probably it wasn't the radio they were thinking about, however. Things happened so fast in the next two hours that it is hard for me to remember them in their correct sequence. I do remember that, through no effort of Jerry's both the radios that had been left behind in the Japanese barracks were in Jerry's hands before the day was over. The radios were brought to him by people who had looted them and wanted them repaired. Naturally there was wild looting at the guards' barracks as soon as the Japanese were gone.

"At dawn a story book ceremony was enacted, and all the time I kept saying to myself, 'This can't be true.' And yet, just as the sun rose, we were singing our own beloved *Star Spangled Banner.* The words have never been so significant, and the flag which had been kept hidden somewhere has never looked so proud or meant so much. People all over the camp cried unashamedly, and two or three women even fainted."*

*Excerpt from Margaret Sams, *Forbidden Family, a wartime memoir,* edited by Lynn Z. Bloom, The University of Wisconsin Press, 1989

(Editor's Note: There was a typhoon going on at the time the Japanese abandoned the camp so most internees stayed inside and ate the food that had been left behind, trying to figure out what to do next. In the meantime, the Japanese returned with more malice than ever.)

After the Japanese soldiers returned they were more suspicious than ever. Someone stole the commandant's bicycle (and other things) while they were gone, which infuriated the commandant. Our friend, Doc Nance said, "I know the man who stole the commandant's bicycle." I thought that was a pretty dumb thing to do, personally. Where could you go in a prison camp on a stolen bicycle? But it turned out that Jerry could use the bike to make a generator for his radio.

The Japanese soldiers were sure there was a radio somewhere in the camp, and they were constantly on the lookout for it. Jerry, my husband, had a very close call with them when he set the radio up with the bicycle (he got away by the skin of his teeth), so we didn't dare play it anymore. Now we had no news of whether the Americans had landed or where the fighting was at that time. We were pretty discouraged and very near the starvation point—the Japanese were giving us even less food than before.

These were the darkest days we'd experienced during our whole incarceration. The Japanese gave us Palai rice (it was considered horse feed) with the husk still on it—about a cupful per day. We tried everything to get the husk off, but nothing worked. We tried grinding it with rocks, rolling it, pounding it, but it wouldn't come off. It was so frustrating! We were starving and we were holding food in our hands—but we couldn't eat it! We were all weak from malnutrition—some people couldn't get up out of bed. Most of us suffered from Beri-Beri so we were in bad shape. I even tried to chew the rice as it was, but it made me sick.

I spent one day, the whole day, peeling the husks off the rice grain by grain. After hours of work, I only had a little handful. I was very depressed and almost without hope. We were convinced we had to escape before it was too late. We were sure we couldn't live much longer under these conditions. I was afraid for my two little children, David 5, and Gerry Ann, 12 months. We decided we would rather take our chances out in the jungle than have them wither away with the swollen bellies and matchstick limbs of those dying of malnutrition.

If the Americans were coming, it seemed like they wouldn't reach us in time, so Jerry and I worked out a plan to go over the fence one night. We told our doctor friend, Doc Nance, and we hoped he would give Gerry Ann a shot of something that would put her to sleep so we could travel without fear of her crying. He advised us against it, but we were determined. He kept saying, "No, you don't want to go yet. The Americans are very close." But all we could see was our children near death, and we had to do something about it.

That night we got everything ready and Doc Nance gave Gerry Ann a shot. But it had the opposite effect! Instead of putting her to sleep Gerry Ann cried all night long. She fussed and cried and didn't sleep at all. I was beside myself with worry and concern—I couldn't sleep either. How could we survive?

What I didn't know at the time was that Ben Edwards and Pete Miles had gone over the fence a few days before. Before going, Pete had made a careful study of the habits of the Japanese soldiers: their early morning exercises, their patrols, their quarters, when and where they were on guard, when and where they were least deployed around the camp, where their guns and ammunition were stored and where they stacked their guns when they went to do their morning exercises. He also made a detailed map of the camp showing exactly where the internees were. He got to the American lines and this was just what they needed to mount an attack.

The Japanese had a horrible ritual every morning. As they did their calisthenics they made a screaming noise that scared me to pieces the first time I heard it. If nothing else ever frightened you, I guarantee that sound they made would get you. It was the sound they made before going into battle.

The afternoon of February 22nd, two planes flew overhead and for the first time I said to myself, "The hell with it, I'm looking up." And what a beautiful sight we saw. Planes were circling around a few miles from us beyond a hill and suddenly they let their bombs go and we saw every bomb dropping. It was a wonderful thing to see at that moment. It didn't matter what the Japanese did to us now — we knew the Americans were there! We were thrilled out of our minds. We found out later the planes were bombing a concentration of Japanese troops at a quarry nearby.

That night was the first time the Japanese didn't

have a roll call in the entire three years we were there. They had gone over to see what damage had been caused by the bombing. The next morning I was up early and wondered if we'd have roll call, suddenly our neighbor called in to us from outside. This man had been a missionary all his life and his parents had been missionaries. He called to Jerry to come outside and Jerry said, "I can't, I don't have my pants on." The response was, "The hell with your pants, come out here." (This was probably the only time he'd ever uttered a swear word.)

We rushed out and there they were. The parachutes were coming down right beside the camp. The American planes were overhead and flying low. One of them had a big sign on the side **"LIBERATION!"**

Jerry ran in to get his telescope (another thing he could have been shot for if the Japanese had known about it) to better see what was going on down by the Japanese barracks. He climbed up into the peak of the barracks but soon rifle shots were flying under him. He decided to get down and dropped like a lead weight onto Charlotte's bed (our neighbor) and broke it all to pieces. She was furious with him for a minute, but he was in high spirits saying, "We're getting out of here! We'll be out of here tonight!" I thought it might take a week for us to be truly liberated. *But in fact, we were out of there in two hours!*

With rifle fire going on all around us Jerry grabbed the Patati (woven reed mat) and yelled for the children and me to jump into the ditch that had been dug alongside of the barracks for drainage. We lived in a section of a long barracks that housed 200 internees.

All at once we heard the American soldiers

marching through singing, "GET READY TO MARCH, GET READY TO MARCH." Those Americans looked like angels to us. They looked like beautiful gods! They were tall. They were strong. They were tan and well fed. We were shrivelled and weak, our spirits almost broken. We hadn't seen any healthy Americans in three years. And they were there to save us! And we were ready!

Of course, we were all in a daze and the paratroopers had trouble getting us to hurry. No one knew where to go. The shooting had hardly died down when I thought of bringing the pictures from my family album that I had saved all this time from our home in Baguio before the war. Jerry and David tore the pictures out of the album and we packed one small bag and a duffle with our remaining things and scurried out to find that some of the barracks were on fire. We learned later that the paratroopers had done it to hurry the evacuation. Suddenly, we could hear the rumbling, rumbling noise of the amtracks—amphibious tanks, our escape vehicles.

The first person we saw in a tank was Doc Nance. He yelled at me, "You see, I told you not to go over the fence!" Well, I was so excited. I think we got into the third amtrack and we headed straight for Laguna de Bay, just beyond sight of the camp. There were about twenty-five of us in this open boat-like tank. We were all elated and hardly aware of the dangers that were still around us. The machine gun on board was firing rounds at snipers up in a tree. We were told to get down on the bottom, but I couldn't do it. I had to watch. I saw them shoot a sniper out of a palm tree, and he fell in the water. Hot shell casings went up David's pants leg and Gerry Ann got burns on her hand. I treated the injuries the best I could with help from the soldiers who also passed out K-rations and chocolate. Our liberators were so generous, you wouldn't believe it. One of them had just gotten his Christmas package (this was Feb. 23rd) and he'd gotten a pipe and tobacco in his box. Since he didn't smoke, he gave it all to Jerry who was delighted.

We found out later the prison at Santo Tomas had been liberated almost 3 weeks earlier and the soldiers had given the internees all the food they wanted. We were told that some of them had died from it. Now, the soldiers had been warned not to give us food since our stomachs couldn't handle rich food after our starvation diet. They weren't supposed to give us their rations, but they couldn't resist, seeing us in such a desperate condition, especially the children.

The amtracks went back and forth across the bay until they got all of us out (2,146 people). It's really amazing! *Not one internee was killed.* and only three people suffered minor injuries. Some people couldn't walk; they had to be carried out, but they got out. We learned later that the American commanders had expected to lose about half of the prisoners during the battle to free us. This was beyond their wildest dreams. It was a miracle. We all got out! The paratroopers didn't lose any men either.

It took us about two hours to cross the bay, and they left us at the New Bilibid Prison (emptied of prisoners) where we stayed a couple of weeks. I couldn't sleep for three nights—I was so excited, full of joy and overwhelmed by what was happening. They fed us carefully — our first meal was celery soup with milk. I'm afraid I was disappointed; I wanted something I could really chew. But gradually we regained our strength.

I remember, there were some iron bedsteads without springs, just the frames in the prison where we stayed. They gave each of us an army blanket and Jerry, being so clever, managed to wrap a blanket around one side of the frame and secure it to the other side so we actually had a bed to sleep on. But I was thinking the whole night, "Here we are on beds and our liberators are outside sleeping on the ground." They were gone early the next morning, moving on to continue the fighting that remained. This was just one thing in their lives—but it's the thing they remember most, they tell us.

The next night we could smell bread baking. Wheew! It was then I knew we were home! There's no way to describe how I felt. We almost didn't make it—and suddenly we were free! At the end we had no more to eat and were facing certain starvation and now we had food. What blessings. For a few days they air-dropped food to us because we were still behind the enemy lines. Then they could come in with trucks with food and supplies.

Jerry was recruited for electronic equipment repair almost immediately so it was a while before we actually left the area. One day when Jerry had gone to Santo Tomas, I met a fellow I had grown up with back home. He was in the navy and he told me about the death of my dear brother, Edward, who was also in the navy. I was very sad about this because we were so close. But I was grateful that he had news of my family from home.

My friend took us to Lingayen, a large military base in the Philippines and every day seemed like Christmas—it was such joy to be out of prison.

We finally headed for home in April of 1945. This was a difficult boat trip. It was very uncomfortable and terribly crowded. We had to wear our life preservers at all times, and the kids had to have theirs on too. I was still weak from malnutrition and had to carry little Gerry Ann around with her life preserver on. The ship had to zig and zag all across the Pacific along with a large convoy of other ships. Weeks later we arrived in SF. Looking out at that skyline, we all had tears in our eyes. "Thank you God, I'm home!" Our lives would never be the same.

The Red Cross wanted to separate us, the men in one area and the women in another. Jerry wouldn't hear of it and left the dock area to find a taxi. Of course, we had no money and no baggage, but he wanted us to have a hotel room that night. I didn't know whether my mother would be coming there or not. I had written her but had received no reply. But when we went down the gang plank (I think we were the last ones off the ship) there was my mother! She met us with her sister and my brother Thomas who was also a navy pilot and my brother Stanley who had been just a little boy when I left. There he was—6'4" tall. It was a thrilling moment!

I found out later that the FBI had notified my mother that I was on this ship coming home and told her she could meet us (of course, they didn't furnish the gas stamps that would enable her to get there), but somehow she made it and we were so happy to be together again.

"Room 40", where 50 men were billeted at Santo Tomas Internment Camp.

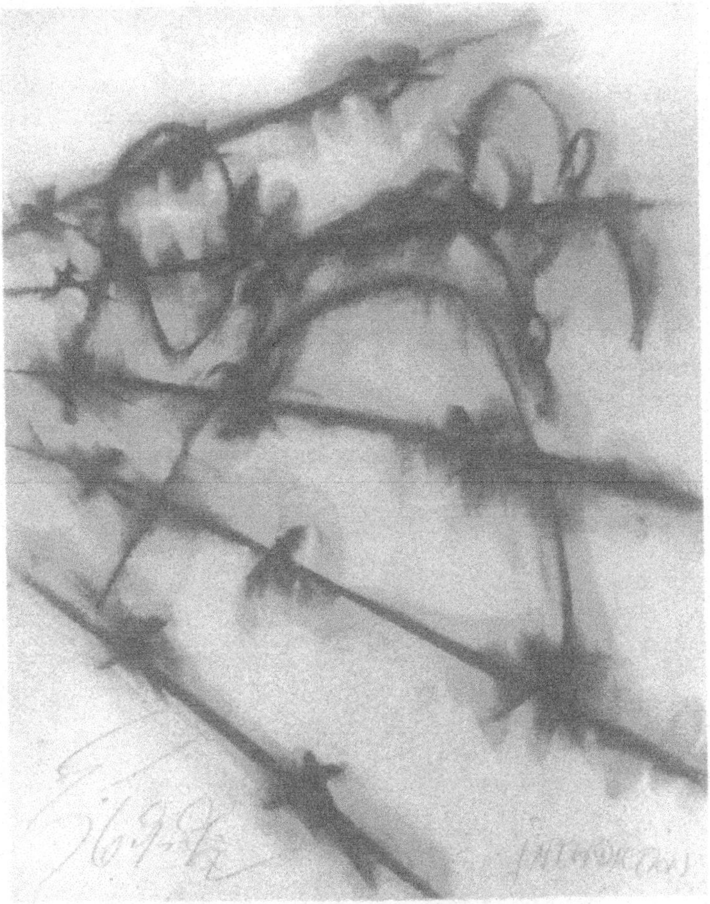

This is What Happens..., #IV, by E.J. Gold,
charcoal on Sennelier Pastel paper, $12^{3}/4$" x 16", 1992.

Jane Wills with her daughter Trudi just after the war.

Jane with her brother, sister and mother in Southern California, 1986. Her mother, father, brother, and sister got the last ship out of Manila in 1942.

Jane Wills

Jane was born in Tonapah, Nevada in 1917 and was raised in Arizona where she met Hugh Wills three years before he took a good job as a mining superintendent in the Philippines. In 1937 she took her first trip away from home, traveling by boat halfway around the world to marry Hugh. Just before arriving in Manila, a typhoon struck the area and her ship was forced to dock in Hong Kong for repairs for four days. She and Hugh were finally united and lived happily until the start of the war.

Mindanao, 1941 –

When the war started, my husband Hugh, my little daughter Trudi (less than a year old), and I lived in the hills outside of Davao on the island of Mindanao at Davao Gold Mine. The only way in or out of this area was by tramway or by airplane. My husband was a mine operator and had been asked by the army to go to a nearby area and help set up demolition work. The army knew the Japanese were on their way. Hugh was assured that he would be replaced in a week but he didn't come home. We got very worried—a week went by and then two weeks and no one replaced him. There was no one to help us in an emergency. He finally returned and told us to pack our things, store them, and go with him to Davao, then to the center of the island where the mining company had some cattle ranches. This we did—we left Davao about 11 o'clock one morning and the Japanese invaded in the evening.

In order to get back after doing the demolition,

Hugh had to escape out the back way, and the army had to escape the same way. My husband Hugh walked through about 300 miles of unexplored territory leading the advanced guard for the army. When he got back he was in very bad shape. He'd contracted dysentery and it took a while for him to get back on his feet. When he felt better, he did everything he could to help the army. He ran the motor pools. Of course it was useless but we did what we could.

When the Japanese took over the island, there was nothing to do but turn ourselves in because the Filipinos were going into the hills with as much ammunition as they could carry, but no food. We knew we couldn't survive in the jungles. I'd been very fortunate in getting quite a bit of canned powdered milk for our little girl, and I didn't want to take a chance of losing it.

For the next 34 months we were prisoners of war. At first we were interned at a dental clinic at Malay-Balay where the Japanese army had an installation. There were just Nipa quonset huts and very hot. These Japanese were the fighting forces and just ignored us, and we ignored them. We couldn't leave, and there was just a small group of us. Then the occupation forces came in and took charge of us while the fighting force moved on. Now everything changed.

The occupation forces gathered all the people from the whole area at Malay-Balay and announced that we'd be leaving in two hours and we could only take two pieces of luggage. Some men had been on the Death March on Mindanao so they had no belongings. They volunteered to carry some of the milk I was saving for my daughter, Trudi. It was so wonderful of them.

The Japanese put us on trucks—somehow or other Hugh was put on one truck and Trudi and I on another. I was anxious that we'd be separated and Trudi was so fidgety, so hard to make behave, and it was so hot! We had no water—I remember, I almost blacked out. They took us to a port on the north coast of Mindanao and put us in a school house. It had been occupied by the troops and it was filthy, so we had to get busy and clean it up as best we could.

While there, the Japanese had the men load a ship with big sacks of rice. Of course we protested saying this was against the Geneva Convention to force us to do hard labor, but they wouldn't listen. While Hugh was working, someone let a big sack of rice down hard on the back of his neck, and he had trouble with his back the rest of his days here.

The commandant had decided that everyone should learn Japanese, so he ordered language classes for all the prisoners. There were separate classes for men, women without children, and for mothers with children. That's where I was with my little girl but she was a "wiggle worm." She was wild and wouldn't settle down. We had three classes and it was havoc trying to quiet these children—it just didn't work. So the commandant issued another order: *everyone would learn Japanese, "the language of the future,"* ***except the mothers with children.***

We got that place cleaned up and as livable as we could make it, and then the Japanese announced, "OK, in two hours, you go." They put us back on a ship and took us all the way around Mindanao Island right back to Davao, where we'd started. There they put us in a convent. It was a two story building. They didn't want us to talk to the Filipinos so they made us stay up on the second floor. The only time we could go down and stay for any length of time was to wash our clothes.

Washing clothes was a matter of doing the best you could to get them clean and then spreading them out over the bushes to dry. Of course you had to watch your laundry or someone would take it. Well, my very dear friend, Vi, said she would watch my little daughter, Trudi, while I went downstairs to wash the clothes.

After a while, of course, Vi wondered how I was getting along. Trudi was getting restless so Vi decided to bring her down to see how I was doing. Trudi was a VERY active little girl and she had in mind to get away from Vi and duck out to the Japanese guards to see if they would give her something to eat. They were sometimes kind to the children, and we never had enough food.

Trudi had such a winning smile, and she would bow and curtsy and show off to the guards and they gave her a little bean cake. Of course, these were dirty with flies and what-have-you and Vi didn't want her to eat it. Around the corner of the guard house she started to take the treat away from Trudi, but suddenly Trudi put up an awful howl. The Japanese guards heard her and came running around the building with their bayonets ready and almost stuck one into Vi because they thought she was trying to take that little cake away from Trudi to eat it herself.

When Vi came back she was so disgusted. She

said, "Oh, I'm never going to take care of your little girl again." Trudi ate the bean cake and got along just fine.

We were there for about three weeks and the Japanese came in one day with the same command: "In two hours you GO." And that's what we did. They took us out on the outskirts of Davao and across the Davao River to an old dance hall called "The Happy Life Blues"—it was filthy but it was our new home. Naturally, we got busy and cleaned it up. There was no sanitation—we had to dig toilets and get along with the little bit of water we had and set up a way to cook food. The Japanese did bring the food, such as it was, and we took care of all the preparation.

This place had so many snakes and bugs, it was terrible. There was a black cobra in the area, and I just hated to walk outside. I wouldn't go anywhere in the dark for fear I'd stumble across it. We were there for two or three months and the Japanese kept bringing in more internees. Each of us had a little square of maybe two or three feet by eight feet of the floor and soon there wasn't enough room for everybody. So the Japanese said that if anyone wanted to go out into the swamp adjoining the property and gather wood and reeds, we could build little shelters of our own off the main building.

We grabbed at the chance. Hugh and our very dear friend, Don Hannings, went into the swamp and brought out the bamboo and some kind of wood that they split to make a floor. Together they built us a little house. My job was to weave the palm fronds to put on the side. I have lived in some very wonderful homes in my life, but I never treasured any of them as much as I treasured that little one room hut. The roof was cogan grass, and when you looked up you could see all these centipedes crawling through the grass roof to catch the bugs. I feared they would drop on us but I never did see one fall. In spite of bugs it was just heaven here after the bedlam of being in the "fish bowl" of this concentration camp with absolutely no privacy.

Hugh's engineer from the mine and his wife Lydia found out where we were and helped us. They would wait until the guards got a little drunk at night, and they'd try to get some food in for us to eat. One day, someone came running in to say that Lydia was at the guardhouse. They wouldn't let me talk to her, but she had brought us (of all things) some laying chickens. We built a little chicken run out of bamboo right by our hut and kept these wonderful laying chickens there. In the morning the camp would have coconut milk on the lugao rice and the residue from the coconut we would feed to the chickens. With that we had a little supplement of eggs to our diet.

Next to our camp, just outside the barbed wire, there was a Japanese farmer who raised chickens. We didn't have any roosters in ours, so in the evening we would open up the little trap door we had in the back, and the Japanese chickens would come right in. We'd rush over and close the gate and keep the chicken—if it was a white one with a few black feathers, we'd pull the black feathers out and keep it. We got quite a few chickens that way; of course, the rooster we'd always put back on the farmer's side because the guards knew we didn't have a rooster. This worked fine, and we didn't get caught.

It was getting close to Christmas, our second Christmas at the "Happy Life Blues," and we were going to have a Christmas program and sing carols. We had made toys for the children like boats or a hobby horse made from bamboo for the boys and little dolls for the girls made out of cogan grass and what-have-you—they were darling. We were planning such a wonderful time, but the Japanese did it again—"In two hours, you GO!"

This time they took us out and put us on a ship in Davao Gulf, and we sat there over Christmas looking at where we'd been. We could see it, "The Happy Life Blues." This was a very low time for us. The ship was filthy and it was full of rats—oh, it was awful! We were on it four or five days until the Japanese formed up a convoy and took us all back around, past Zamboanga, into the sea in between the outer islands on our way to Manila.

When we got to Cebu (our ship was very slow with no markings on it saying we were prisoners of war), the rest of the convoy left us—and there we were like sitting ducks. I was very fearful that we'd be attacked by U.S. submarines (we had heard that some ships had been sunk that way).

We made it over to Manila and they put us in the camp at Santo Tomas which had been a university. They put my husband on the fifth floor of the main building with the other men and put me with the mothers and children. It was very crowded. Everyone had been living there for almost two years. The only space left was of course in the worst spot—we had to be among the mothers who were going out with the Japanese and not taking care of their children. Well, it was just terrible. There was bedlam day and night. After the anxiety of the ship ride, I couldn't get any rest here either and was in awful shape.

Before the war, I had been up at Baguio on Luzon island and some of my friends from Benguet Gold Mines were here at Santo Tomas; they had a room of their own. Of course, my friends were very selective about who they would let live in their room, and they invited me to move in because one of the ladies was going to move out. The Japanese let people build little shacks and huts, and she and her children were moving into one of the huts. Well, when I moved in it was just heaven. Here the mothers took care of their children like I took care of my little girl and everything was organized and clean.

It was very difficult for my husband where he was located. He had been sick a number of times and it was hard for him to climb up and down five flights of stairs. At about this time, the Japanese sent the single men out into the country to the agricultural extension of the university, Los Baños, to build another camp. We decided that we should try to go to this new camp because he would not be able to go climbing up and down stairs very much longer.

So we were transferred to Los Baños out in the country, and there we were interned in Nipa quonset huts, a big long shed-like building, divided down the middle with divisions like horse stalls on each side. We had our spot there and a chance to be back together as a family and this was a big help. My husband was in charge of this barracks, and if anyone had a problem or a grievance they would bring it to him. Then he would take it to the Council which we elected. In any emergency, he was to see to the safety of each of us in the quonset. He was very concerned for our safety should any fighting occur so he went out to the embankment and dug out a place where we could go for shelter in case we'd need it.

Everything went along pretty well. The men who had originally established the camp had also planted a great big garden. Just when it was time to harvest the crop, the Japanese built a fence around it and took all the vegetables and only gave us our regular ration. We were so disappointed. We never had much to eat. In the morning we had rice, and sometimes it had worms in it. We didn't get coconut milk anymore. For lunch we'd get some kind of a vegetable with rice and the same for dinner—the portions were very small. We were always hungry.

Once the camp got a lot of meat. There was an epidemic among the hogs, and the Japanese sent in all this pork. We decided to try it and cooked it a very long time and no one had ill effects. It was good!

One nice thing happened. There was a man I used to play bridge with in Davao who was in that camp. He was a good friend of my husband's too and he came over and invited me to play with his group each week. We'd play all afternoon with the stakes of maybe an egg or a banana. I never knew where these treats were coming from, but I didn't ask questions. Merle and I frequently won the set. Merle was always a gentleman and gave me the prize to take back to my family.

So I knew that some food was coming in. Sometimes, my husband would talk privately with a friend and not let me in on it. He said, "Things are progressing, but if you are questioned, it's better if you know nothing about it. That way you can't get hurt."

The Japanese came in, and we could hear shells and artillery fire. They said the American forces were coming, and they would let us go free. The Japanese went to Manila and during that time we got coconut milk, eggs, and meat for the children and the sick and we got coconut, bananas, and meat for the rest of the camp.

There was a rice mill outside the camp and down the railroad tracks. There was a fire there and our men went down and carried sacks of rice on their backs and distributed it to everyone in the camp. The only problem was that it hadn't been milled and was nearly impossible to get the husk off, so we couldn't eat it.

We were free from the Japanese for about a week. We found out then that there were two radios in the camp. The young, single men had them, and they would pump a bicycle to get the current up to play the radio. That's how some news was coming in. I heard that some people were getting in and out of the camp, though I never found out how they did it. We were so glad the Japanese had left but weren't sure what would happen next.

A few nights later I heard many trucks rumbling in (of course there was a blackout). There wasn't any shouting or joy or singing and I thought, "Oh, no—the Japs are back!" And sure enough the Japanese had come back and taken over the camp. Of course, some of the people would not accept that we were prisoners again and started to walk out. The Japanese shot at them. One man didn't stop and they killed him. This made people fall in line.

It was very difficult then. The food situation was impossible. During the time in Santo Tomas, we had received a Red Cross package. One each for my husband and myself, and little Trudi received half a package and a Care Package. This Care Package was set up for a young lady, and it had such wonderful things in it as make up, cold cream and, of all things, Kotex. This was something that was impossible to get here. I looked at it and knew that I could trade it for food. So I traded the whole package for food for Trudi. We had just about used up the Red Cross package at Los Baños. Before the Japanese left for Manila, they were trading us extra food in exchange for valuables like jewelry. I still had my wedding ring, and my husband still had a watch. We decided we had to have extra food and wanted to try to trade the ring and watch. We wanted to trade for anything we could get. The Japanese took the watch, dropped it and broke it. My ring had diamonds that were inset so they couldn't scratch on glass to prove they were real diamonds, so they wouldn't accept it.

A friend, Mona Raymond, had a beautiful watch that had rubies and diamonds in it and she traded it for food, getting two kilos of rice, two kilos of corn, some tea and some sugar. Bless her dear heart, she insisted that she give some of it to us for my husband who was in bad shape and little Trudi. Another dear friend, who'd been in on the negotiating when the Japanese dropped Hugh's watch, came and gave us some of their food that they had traded for a diamond ring. My heart still just melts when I think of these wonderful friends who shared with us when they too were starving.

After the Japanese came back, they were very, very cruel. They cut back on our rations and gave us even less than before—we had only two meals a day. Half the camp would get rice and camoti leaves (like sweet potato plants) and the other half got rice (without salt) and water. Then at the second meal we'd get the opposite meal — that wasn't enough to keep us going. We still had this unhulled rice we'd gotten, and we decided we'd better use it.

There were a lot of missionary families in this camp, and one family had a grinder. They'd let people use the grinder for a portion of their rice. Then you could break off the husk and winnow it and cook it. Of course, any prolonged use of this crude rice, normally given to cattle, and it would cut your stomach to pieces. But we went ahead and supplemented our food this way.

I was always so thankful that the supply of milk for little Trudi kept up. She had almost 3/4 of a cup most everyday. I do hope it helped. I didn't ever sell any of this milk or trade it, but if there was a case of dire need or extreme illness, I just gave a can of powdered milk to them in a number of cases. But as a general rule I gave it to my little girl, and the poor little thing was so hungry. Here we'd sit down to a meal of rice on a tin plate, and Trudi would gobble hers down right away, and my husband would look at me, and I'd look at him and we'd go over and dish a spoonful of ours onto her plate. That's not easy to do when you're starving—it's unbelievable how hungry we got.

We heard rumors that the Americans were getting closer. We could hear the guns and the shelling, but we didn't know really what was happening. All of a sudden the Japanese came through the camp searching for a radio. They decided to search our camp while we were at roll call. They started tearing our little cubicles all to pieces. They had machine guns trained on us, but we protested. I put Trudi right in front of me to protect her. We told the Japanese that if they wanted to search our places they could, but we had to be there. And they did, they let us watch—but they tore some of the places all to pieces. We didn't have anything so they poked around in ours, and that was about it.

The Japanese were back about three weeks when one morning at the crack of dawn we heard many planes overhead. We looked up and saw the sky full of parachutes coming down just south of us. On one plane there were great big letters—I'll never forget it—saying "**RESCUE.**" About that time the bullets began flying, and my husband had us go into the little place he had dug, and then he went back in to see that everyone in the barracks was protected in some way. Well, when these parachutes started coming down, Sandy Begiry (who hadn't been able to walk for the last month and who lived in the stall next to us with his wife) went outside and did the Highland Fling (he was a Scotsman). A happy, happy thing! Everyone was elated.

The bullets were still coming so we just had to stay in our hiding places. Oh, what a wonderful sight it was when the American soldiers came in. They told us, "**Grab your things—we're taking you out**!" And they did. We took what we could with us, and they put us on these amphibious tanks and headed us out. There was still shooting and fighting all around. At one point I looked down at Trudi who had brought a handful of rice and a funny little doll I had made her — it was very precious to her and gave her a great deal of comfort.

In the amtracks we went down to the lake then headed across to New Bilibid Prison on the other side of the bay. My husband, who was very patriotic, decided to stay and help get everyone out, so he sent Trudi and me on ahead. He stayed and was on one of the last amphibious tanks to go out of there. It was a beautiful operation. A tank corps came across the lake to the north of the camp and held the line there. The U.S. army soldiers came through the camp and went up into the hills to defend from there. The paratroopers held the territory to the south and the lake was on the other side.

They kept us at Bilibid Prison because the Japanese were retreating through Los Baños. It's amazing that none of the internees were killed or seriously injured in this operation. One man who was so thin that his skin hung down in folds, got hit by a bullet, but it went around and around and did no serious damage.

At New Bilibid, the American army had set up soup kitchens. You know, we couldn't eat normal meals because we'd been starved for so long. We had to be careful to eat a little at a time. But they did give us chocolate and of course, little Trudi was out there bowing and curtsying to these soldiers to get more chocolate.

It's a wonder she didn't turn into a hunk of chocolate.

We were housed at New Bilibid until the Americans could secure the island. Then they took us on trucks to Manila and put us on a troop ship, the Eberly, to go home. That trip home was unbelievable. We were about four decks down, and I had to try to carry Trudi up and down the stairs. I was so weak that I could hardly do it. We would just have to sit down on the deck to rest — my bones were right next to the skin with no padding so it was very uncomfortable. That was a difficult trip, but we were free! The other good thing was the food. We got good food for the first time in three years!

When we got back to the states, a big convention was going on in San Francisco so they landed us in Los Angeles. Then we went to our home where my mother was in Arizona. One interesting thing had happened— remember I mentioned that I used to play bridge in Davao? Well, a friend of mine, Lucy Brown, was married to the British Vice Consul there and we used to play bridge. When there was an exchange of prisoners in 1942, Lucy and her husband got out of the Philippines. Lucy knew a man who was the former mill superintendent at Davao Gold Mines, and although she didn't have my address in the states, she did know that this man knew my husband's people. She got the address and when she was in the states on her way to England, she contacted Hugh's family and told them where we were and how we were. So both our families did have word about us during the early part of the war.

Of course, periodically the Japanese had us write letters home and oh, how we labored over those letters!

But of course, they never sent them. But we tried....

Now, what did I learn from this war? I think I really learned to appreciate everything. Before, I took things for granted. But when I got to the point of dreaming about just having something to eat from my former garbage can.... I admit, before the war I was wasteful. I learned to be very careful and to use everything—to try to help the environment and the country. The war made me really appreciate people. When you get right down to the point of having nothing left, no medicine, no food, nothing—something changes inside. I'm thankful I had a strong faith and trust in God.

"Gigi" Poston's watercolor sketch of Santo Tomas.

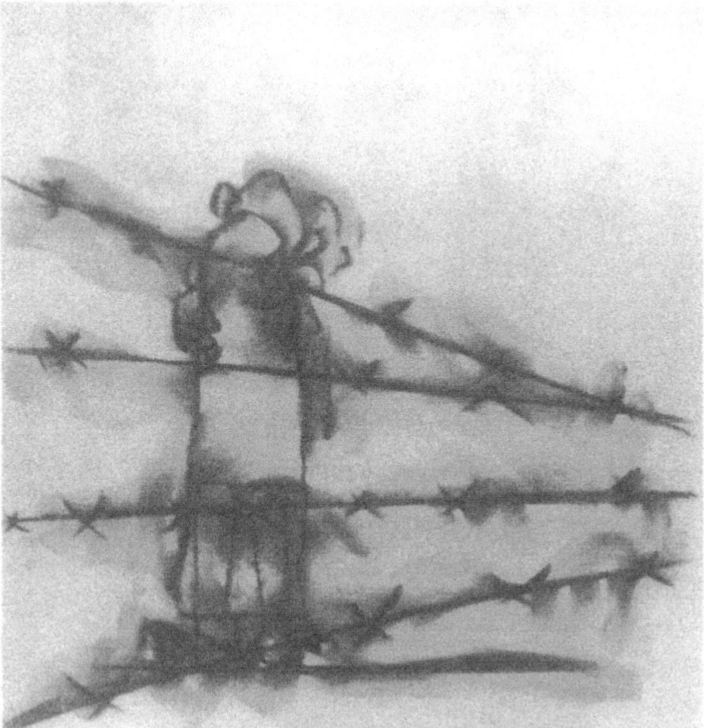

This is What Happens..., #V, by E.J. Gold,
charcoal on Sennelier Pastel paper, $12^{3}/4$" x 16", 1992.

Sascha Jean Weinzheimer in 1943

Sascha Jean Weinzheimer Jansen in 1994

Sascha Jean Jansen

Sascha Jean was born and raised in the Philippines on her grandfather's sugar plantation, Calamba Sugar Estates. Her father was German/Hawaiian and her mother was German/Tahitian. She had polio when she was 18 months old and every year and a half went to San Francisco for reconstructive surgery on her legs. She had to have physical therapy and get fitted for the new braces after each surgery. Her father would meet them in the States and the family would go on vacation.

June, 1939 –

I was seven years old and my parents took me and my sister on a vacation to Europe to visit my father's relatives. We were left with my nursemaid (my Filipino "amah") at the home of my aunt and uncle in Speyer, Germany, while my parents went to different places in Europe on business and vacationing.

Unfortunately, my sister and I didn't have our own passports since we were on mother's passport. Normally this would be fine, but the war was threatening, and while my mother was in Genoa getting ready to come and pick us up so we could take the boat to New York, the borders closed. We couldn't get out of Germany and my parents couldn't get to us.

They decided that my cousin would take us and our amah to Switzerland, right on the border, and somehow we would be able to meet my father in Basel. We spent a terrifying time on the train where we weren't allowed to speak English because there were soldiers everywhere and if they found out that we were foreigners, without passports, we'd be arrested. We spent hours every day changing trains, dodging officials, hiding here and there so we wouldn't be detected.

I don't know how we did it, but we got to my father in Basel and he was able to get us back to Genoa by having my mother hide out in a hotel room while he got us through customs with her passport. We were booked on the Contessa de Savoia and had loaded all our baggage on it when we found out that it wouldn't sail—all passenger ships were cancelled. My father was very resourceful, however, and discovered a freighter, the President Monroe, would be sailing the next day. He negotiated our passage using his prestige as a frequent commercial shipper of the sugar from his plantation with the President Lines. The amazing thing was, he even got an agreement to take another 250 displaced people who'd been left stranded in Europe and couldn't get home. They were all sitting around in the port at the docks and father said, "Well, if you're going to take us, what about all these people who have no way to get home?" The shipping agent said, "Definitely not, we have no accommodations for passengers. This is a freighter!"

My father insisted and everyone agreed that we'd all sleep on the deck, just to get back home. This was one of those rough Atlantic crossings, but we did it. We all slept on the deck and tried to stay out of the way of the seamen. My father and the other men took on the job of waiters to serve meals to these unexpected passengers. Halfway across we were stopped by a U-Boat, that signaled our ship to stop. The captain did not let on that he had passengers so this was a dangerous moment. All of us were sent below and had to be totally quiet. There were some other children on board, and we were all scared, but we tried to stay as quiet as we could. Their crew could have detected if there were many people on board if we hadn't stayed quiet.

The U-Boat came alongside and this was a tense half hour. Luckily they didn't board us. They believed whatever the captain told them, and we proceeded on to New York. At the dock in New York, the press was there to welcome us. They made a big to-do about it, and we had our pictures on the front page of the paper. Of course we didn't have any luggage, but we were thankful we'd gotten out of there alive. We continued on across the country and took another ship from San Francisco back to the Philippines.

Life for us was pretty normal; the war in Europe seemed a long way away, but suddenly in late 1941, it came to our doorstep. The Japanese attacked, and the Philippines quickly fell. I was supposed to go to San Francisco again in early 1942 for the surgery and new braces, but we were put in Santo Tomas prison camp during the war, and by the end of the war I had of course outgrown the special shoes and braces. My legs were as bad as they were when the doctors first started to operate. I had to start all over again after the war with more reconstructive surgery.

We had heard rumblings and rumors about the Japanese military aggressiveness even before Pearl Harbor. The Japanese took over Indonesia, Nanking, and Manchuria, so the attack on the U.S. didn't come as a total surprise. Their idea was to build a "Greater East Asia Co-Prosperity Sphere," as they called it. They wanted to take over the whole Far East and then take on America.

Carl and Shelly Mydans were visiting us when the war started, a photographer/writer team from Time-Life. They were doing a picture story of sugar plantation life in the Philippines, among other things. They immediately switched to being war correspondents and later were captured and put in prison with us. Later they were sent to prison in Japan and then repatriated. I suspect the U.S. government wanted them home to give crucial information about the Philippines. Carl was the first man into Santo Tomas prison with the liberation troops in 1945. He was extremely important to the liberation forces for his first hand information.

The Japanese attacked Cavite, Manila's port, the same day as they bombed Pearl Harbor. (They bombed Borneo, Hong Kong, and Singapore the same day, too, but not many people mention this.) It was Monday, December 8, 1941 (because we were across the International date line), and I was in Manila, one hour away from home at my physical therapy session with Mrs. Shay, my amah, and chauffeur (also with Gen. Lim's daughter who had polio, too). We had to work our way back to the plantation avoiding rubble and refugees, and we could hear the bombs in the background. We were scared but I didn't really know what was happening. The amah and chauffeur were talking a mile a minute in Tagalog, but I didn't know what they were saying. I was just glad when we got back to the house.

We were waiting to see what would happen, and within a few days, the Japanese were bombing our plantation. We had railroad tracks to our place which were used for shipping sugar, but they were bombing anything that looked strategic and railroads were a good target. The U.S. Army was trying to defend the territory and even set up an airfield in our cane fields. They disguised it during the day and used it for some raids of their own, but soon this had to be abandoned and my father realized we had better get out.

After much organizing, we all piled in the car and headed for Manila. There, we managed to get a room in the Bay View Hotel with other American and British refugees. We got word that the Japanese troops were coming in and later had to watch as they brought down the American flag and raised the Japanese flag. This was a sad moment for all of us and the beginning of a long, difficult period, a different reality for all of us.

We were told to stay in the hotel and not leave—they would come around for inspection. My brother was only three months old, my sister was three years old, and I had these heavy braces on. When they came, they made me wait on them and were crude and rough with us. They announced that the mothers with small children could stay out, but everyone else had to go to prison. My father had to go.

They put us in cars with eight other women and children and many of the amahs who didn't want to leave. They took us to the home of the Kneedlers who owned the Bay View Hotel. We bivouacked there for a while, and the Japanese officers took over the Hotel. The

Japanese were going door to door picking up all aliens and putting them in Santo Tomas prison, but we were given arm bands to show that it was OK for us to go out and get food at the store. Presumably, we wouldn't get picked up, but they were very aggressive, and they would scream and yell at any of us in the street. My mother was worried and told all the children not to ever answer the door. One day, I opened the door when someone was knocking and a gruff Japanese soldier marched in. He reached over and tweaked one of my breasts and laughed—I felt terribly humiliated and cried for hours. It took me a long time to forget the pain of that incident.

After that, my mother said we needed to move to a safer place, and she went to the Assumption Convent nearby asking if we could take refuge there. The Mother Superior said no, it would be too dangerous for them until she heard our name, Weinzheimer. She remembered that grandfather had been lending them his beach house every year for many years for their annual retreats. Then she relented. My mother said that all eight women and their children (close to twenty-five people) should come too and again the mother superior said no. But after more conversation, she agreed. Now, all of us came to live at the convent.

We tried to maintain a very low profile, but it was hard. We all lived in one room and the kids were screaming all the time and some people were sick. We knew we couldn't continue there for long, and the nuns finally asked us to leave because the Japanese wanted them to reopen their school. My mother was determined. She went to a French convent, St. Paul, nearby and asked them for help. They hid us for a while with one other family, and the rest went into Santo Tomas.

The Japanese were starting to send their own nuns to teach at these schools for language classes—it was inevitable. I wanted to go to school and did so for a while, but soon my mother put her foot down. It was too dangerous on the outside.

Every two to three weeks we'd go and visit my father. It took a long time to get there in a horse drawn cart, but we wanted to see him. We brought him food and supplies if we could. The almost 3,000 internees at Santo Tomas were allowed to set up their own government, a committee to manage their own affairs as prisoners of war. For the first year and a half the Japanese let the front gate be open to visitors once a week for a few hours, and many of the people on the outside and some of the forme Filipino servants of the internees came and brought food. Sometimes they could visit for ten minutes or so.

We survived outside for almost a year, and finally my mother said we should go ourselves inside the camp. We felt we'd be safer inside since many atrocities were still being committed and many women were being beaten and raped; others were being brutally murdered. Sometimes my mother would send me to Mrs. Shay's with my amah for my exercises, and I had to pass a building that had been taken over by the Japanese soldiers. They would sit around outside and harass people going by. Usually I tried to go around in back of this building, but one day I saw that the soldiers were torturing a Filipino boy who had been doing errands for them. There was an old bathtub out in front, and they were drowning him. We were terrified and went running back to St. Paul's to my mother. After that we didn't go outside of the convent again.

We felt much safer inside the camp, and we were glad to be with my father again. Some people set up little tables to sell things that had been brought in from the outside—maybe a cigarette or some kind of vegetable or even a sanitary napkin (much prized by the female inmates). These enterprises were tolerated at first by the Japanese.

Each prisoner had some kind of job and worked at it for some period each day. My dad was head of the kitchen sanitation. The women and kids were part of the vegetable detail. At first we cut off parts of the vegetables as we did at home and discarded them, but when the Japanese military took over the camp, our rations were cut in half and the food was very inferior. Now, we got wormy vegetables and didn't cut anything off—we ate worms with pleasure. They were a good source of protein and filling. Soon we had no vegetables at all so some of us were out of a job. The military closed the front gate, and no visitors were allowed after that. There was no milk and nothing extra for the babies. We got only rice gruel (*lugao*—watery rice) and not a full scoop of that. We'd have that for breakfast and an even smaller quantity for lunch and dinner with a watery soup concoction. One time the bulletin board did announce "Duck Soup for Dinner!" That was true but it was kind of a joke. There was a duck pond in the back and twice we had duck soup. There were possibly eight ducks in the pond and they'd be killed to make the soup. But by the time you serve 3,000 people you have to stretch those eight ducks a long ways. We could barely taste anything in the warm water.

There were classes for the kids when we first came in since there were many teachers among the internees. That was fine for a while; the classes were held out under the trees. Then the classes were moved to the roof of one of the buildings and the only access was walking up eight flights of stairs. I just wasn't strong enough to make it up there, and with the poor food we got, it used up too much vital energy to climb. Soon none of the kids went to the classes anymore.

My mother decided to have me sit down and write a diary of what was happening to us in the camp. We always had to hide it because the Japanese had forbidden that anyone keep a diary or notes on the situation there.

At first we were put in the big section of women and children with about forty people to a room on little cots that were placed right next to each other. It was awful. Kids were screaming all night and many were sick. No one could get any sleep and disease was rampant. The Japanese let some families build their own shanties to relieve the congestion in the dorms. These were built using palm leaves of nipa and bamboo, and they let my father build one for us. We grew patola vines and a little banana tree next to it, and it was very nice. Eventually we were forced to eat these vines and palm leaves so the shanty looked pretty bad at the end. We even ate the whole banana tree, stock and all. By the end we had cut most of the shack up for firewood.

I started my period in prison when I was ten years old, but I only had it for four months. All the women in the camp eventually stopped getting their periods because of malnutrition. Until then, though, we had to scrounge rags and diapers, fold them to the proper thickness, sew them crudely, wear them, undo them, wash them by hand, hang them up to dry and use them over again. Little wonder we were thrilled when our periods stopped. When we started eating again, after our liberation, it took some of us five weeks to start up again.

For everything we did in camp we had to wait in line. There were lines for food, of course, lines for washing up, lines for the bathroom, lines for showers, lines for everything. I was in charge of emptying the potty bucket twice a day and had to take it to the toilets and stand in line there. My mother's job was standing at the toilet entrance, handing out two little pieces of toilet paper to each person going in. Sometimes I helped her out there.

My father's job in the kitchen didn't mean that we could get extra food. He was in charge of sanitation and had to keep other people from stealing. He was very careful and very fair. We had to stand in line just like everybody else, and each portion was monitored. You had to have a ticket and if you were getting food for your family, the ticket had to be punched that many times so you wouldn't try to come back for more. My dad was always working the hardest, yet he would always give us kids a spoonful from his plate. He had a big heart, but we didn't realize he was suffering himself from hunger.

People inside the camp who had been bank presidents or industrial magnates were scrounging for food in the worst way. I saw them going through garbage cans for food and rummaging outside the Japanese headquarters hoping to find something to eat. One lady had a two year old baby and would tie a rope onto it and lower it into the garbage pit to pick up food. She would point at what she wanted, and the baby would get it for her. My father told us never to do that. Some of the kids would go around the Japanese sentries (some of them liked kids), and sometimes they would give out cigarettes or treats. My mother told me never to do that so we always stayed away. She said it was a disgrace to beg.

Our day started very early with roll call. We were taught how to bow in the traditional Japanese fashion over and over again. When they called your name you had to bow correctly or get kicked or bayoneted or hit on the head.

People did a lot of strange things. When the liberating forces came into camp, Lt. Abiko was the Japanese in charge. He ran into the plaza and was seen ready to throw a grenade. A U.S. soldier from behind a tank saw this and shot him. Immediately some male prisoners saw what happened and dragged Abiko into a building. There they found the grenade in his hand and took his knife, slitting his throat from ear to ear and his belly. He had been so mean and cruel to all of us for so long, we were not sorry he died in this manner.

How did the war change me? The experience during the war never leaves my mind for very long. I don't dwell on it to be sure, however, there are daily occurrences that remind me of incidents during our imprisonment. For one thing, I always feel like I'm on the outside looking in. I especially felt that way when we came back to the states after the war. I met kids who'd never stopped being kids. But during the war I had to stop being a kid way before my time. I had to be grown up and get smart at an early age. I had to develop a survival instinct. I saw people decapitated; I saw blood and guts on the ground, arms and legs and bodies. We had a game that we used to play, "I saw…" We'd play one-upmanship with other kids. Each would tell what "I saw" and find who could tell the worst story. The awful thing about this game was it was all true!

Even now when I go to work and see the coffee pot is almost empty, I will make a fresh pot. Taking out the old grounds to throw away reminds me of a time just before liberation. At the end my mother almost died. She weighed only 73 pounds, and she's 5'8" tall. She couldn't get up out of bed. She would have died in a few days, and my father decided to try one last remedy. He bought a pound of Hills Bros. Coffee on the Black Market for $350.00 in IOU form. He knew the coffee would give her strength, and he gave it to all of us. Maybe it would buy her time for a few more days. We re-used the grounds over and over and over again. We had coffee left over when the liberation troops came in, and we shared it with them. My mother survived because of it, I'm sure. She had nursed my brother until he was three years old, and he was always chubby, but it depleted her strength terribly. The adrenaline from the coffee gave her the energy to jump out of bed when those American soldiers stormed in to save us. This is a daily reminder when I feel I am "wasting the coffee grounds."

When I fix dinner and peel a turnip or carrot or potato, cutting off the ends to serve the best part, I can't throw any of it away. I save it in a container in the freezer, and when it's full, I make soup from it. These are everyday things that I can't forget. I developed a sense of self-reliance and a bigger imagination as a result of my captivity. I had to use all the stuff that was inside me to survive. How am I going to get the most out of this or that without hurting anybody else? I would always ask myself that. The self-assurance that I have today comes from those experiences. The ability to handle problems—when I'm faced with a problem, I go up and around it, I go in and under it until it's solved, and then I go on to the next. There's always a solution to every problem, believe me. I find a solution and do away with it. It's an intuitive or visceral response I have that's built in. Because of my experiences, too, I have greater tolerance and compassion for others. I can survive a lot of things and this instinct doesn't leave me. In my family, we all have a very high level of humor—we enjoy humor and have kept our sense of it. It has come in handy so many times—I can't do without it.

Just before the war my mother wrote and asked my grandfather in the states to let us come to visit, because it looked like the Japanese were going to start something. He answered that it was a foolish idea and it was just her imagination—her place was with her husband. She and the children should stay there and not worry. When he found out what happened to us, he became ill and literally died of a broken heart.

Quite a few months before Pearl Harbor we learned that the military dependents had been evacuated from the Philippines. Of course, this was a clue that something was going to happen. American and European businessmen went to the High Commissioner's office and asked what was going on and should they plan to evacuate too. They were told that there was no threat, but there was an elaborate evacuation plan in place should we need it—there was nothing to worry about. After the war the High Commissioner, Francis Sayer, testified to the Congress that there were never evacuation plans. Roosevelt felt if we all pulled out it would undermine Philippine morale, and, besides, the President was more concerned with the war in Europe. We could have been spared all that. We were hostages of our own government so the USA would look good. There are organizations working right now to right the wrongs that were committed at that time. This was a hostage situation by our own government all the way around. Make no mistake about it.

As a young adult, my sister Doris developed a severe condition of paranoid schizophrenia. In fact we had to suppress her hysteria by stuffing things in her mouth when the Japanese guards terrorized us—we did that so she wouldn't scream. She always had terrible nightmares for years after the war. My mother suffered malnutrition and almost died and in spite of this she nursed my brother until he was almost three years old. My own leg and back muscles deteriorated early due to malnutrition and exacerbated my post-polio condition.

• • •

The following is from a screenplay in progress by Sascha Jean Jansen:

PIGTAILS IN PRISON

FADE IN:

EXTERIOR: LIMOUSINE DRIVING ON A ROAD—DUSK

Aerial view of traveling limousine flanked by sugar cane fields and golf course. It continues past large swimming pool, club house, tennis courts, and a few well-endowed homes. A huge sugar mill is seen in the distance. JEANIE: (young woman voice-over)

As I remember, growing up on a sugar plantation in the Philippines was something short of heaven. We opened Calamba Sugar Estates to visiting dignitaries and guests, so the footpaths of the well-heeled were in constant use.

Our home was large and airy with tropical foliage, orchids, and water-lilied fish ponds with magnificent Japanese koi fish. It was a romantic's dream.

Because I was the only child of my age on the plantation, I entertained imaginary friends with lavish tea parties in my nipa palm playhouse. If they couldn't be conjured up on any given day, I would corral my amah, the cook, and sometimes my dear gardener into sitting down to tea. They sat there with the patience of Job, even though, I suspect, they longed to be elsewhere.

When I was a baby, I contracted Infantile Paralysis, which left me to lug about long, heavy leg braces. Every other year, we would sail to San Francisco for yet another round of surgery on my legs. Religiously, I was driven into Manila three times a week for much-needed exercises with a miracle worker named Mrs. Schay, and every day I would go horseback riding with Peter Perkins, a handsome, young polo player, who not only taught me how to ride with all that metal, but helped me to nurture my dreams of being the first woman constable, on horseback, of course.

Now that you know a little about me, I shall begin my story on December 7, 1941—exactly two months before my ninth birthday.

CUT TO:

INTERIOR: CHAUFFEUR-DRIVEN LIMOUSINE—DUSK

A man and woman in cocktail attire sit in the back seat. CARL, short, dark-complexioned, and wiry, is fussing with a camera and film, looking through lenses, and blowing off lint. SHELLY is amusingly pert, with dark, bobbed hair and flashing eyes. She writes vigorously, breaks a pencil, cusses, and reaches for another.

A column of jeeps, loaded with American soldiers with guns, passes the limo going in the opposite direction. Shelly gives Carl a concerned look and fans herself.

SHELLY:

That's more khaki than I care to see—I feel like a piker, covering an elegant dinner party with all this trouble brewing with Japan. Any inkling of the guest list?

CARL:

Consider this a respite, love. If you've done your homework, you know the Weinzheimer parties read like Who's Who.

The limo enters a gated entrance. They address the guards.

CARL:

Carl and Shelly Mydans, *Time* and *Life*...we're expected.

SHELLY: *(checking landscape)*

The old man, Louie, just retired, was quite an empire builder, I understand—started all this in Hawaii.... Oh, God, Carl, what breathtaking orchids...going to hate to go home in two weeks. *The limo stops under the portico. Carl playfully slaps her behind as the houseboy helps them out of the car.*

CARL:

You may get your wish, honey...we may be reporting from the trenches by then.

EXTERIOR VERANDA

WALTER and SASCHA are seen welcoming guests coming up the steps. Walter is in his 30s, a handsome example of his Hawaiian-German lineage. Charm and inner strength exude from his well-built, tanned physique. His wife, Sascha, a striking brunette of elegant fragility, complements him. She is obviously enjoying her role as hostess.

WALTER: *(addressing the Mydans)*

Welcome! Mabuyah! Looking at you two, one would think you were working tonight! *(They laugh.)*

SASCHA:

I trust your room at the clubhouse is to your liking. If you need a rest from all that gear, please use the guest room. Come, let's start introductions.

(To one of the houseboys)

Guillermo, drinks for the Mydans!

INTERIOR, LARGE, AIRY TROPICAL HOME

Ceiling fans revolve quietly over well-groomed men and women dressed in evening attire befitting the tropics. Barefoot Filipino houseboys in white are passing drinks and canapes. A six-piece orchestra softly plays "Deep Purple," and bartenders are kept busy at their stations.

CUT TO:

INTERIOR CHILD'S BEDROOM—NIGHT

Two Filipino servants enter the bedroom. The amah is excitable as she looks under beds, in closets, and out of windows. She lifts up a pair of leg braces from the floor and waves them at the houseboy.

ESPERANZA:

I told her…go to sleep already, no more getting out of bed, tsk, tsk, tsk. Sasampalingkita! She is gone some more…Jesus, Maria, Josep…

She quickly makes the sign of the cross, then pushes the houseboy out the door and follows him.

DISSOLVE TO:

EXTERIOR VERANDA

A slight eight year old girl dressed in a thin nightgown is seen crawling behind some ferns and disappears behind a large peacock chair. She has short brown hair, and her large green eyes show a hint of mischievous amusement.

CUT TO:

INTERIOR VERANDA

The tables are exquisitely appointed with candlelight and gardenias. Houseboys are replenishing ice water and wine among the dinner guests. The air is peppered with conversation as the camera pans the dining area.

...If Japan rears its military head, I assure you, we'll give you plenty of notice to....

...The Philippine Navy only consists of eight torpedo boats and four of them are under construction....

...At this moment in Washington, the Japanese have sent an ambassador to....

...We're headed for a war, I am under no delusions....

...I couldn't get near MacArthur on that one...had to send copy back to the main office....

...We should have been out of here when the military dependents were given 24-hour notice a month ago....

...they wouldn't dare touch us...after all...WE'RE AMERICANS!

The camera stops panning at Sascha's table. She is flanked by an Archbishop of the Catholic Church and a commando-physiqued young man, GEORGE WOODS.

SASCHA:

I'm thrilled you enjoyed the curry, Your Excellency. Jesus outdid himself tonight.

ARCHBISHOP:

I may steal this recipe for my housekeeper back in Chicago. My visiting prelates from the missions will be jubilant.

George rises from the table, holds out his hand to Sascha, and addresses the prelate.

GEORGE:

With your permission, Your Excellency....

George and Sascha stroll out onto the dance floor.

SASCHA:

Those snipe hunting trips away from the plantation don't fool Walter and I, George. How long has military intelligence kept you under wraps?

GEORGE: *(chuckling)*

Ah, you're forgetting, Sascha, my PR post takes up all my time...bring back snipes, don't I? No G-man tactics for me. Say, I have a present for Jeanie....

SASCHA:

Mmmmm, you change subjects faster than a mother changes diapers. *They dance off.*

The camera pans to ROSEY ROSENBAUM, a 40-ish, craggy-faced Jewish lady with gnarled, arthritic hands displaying lavish rings. She is in chatty conversation with her dance partner, GENERAL CARLOS ROMULO. Both are extremely short.

ROSEY:

...know exactly what your wife would look good in, General. Send over one of her evening gowns...I will design a stunner—leave it to me!

ROMULO:

Your reputation as a couturier is an asset to the P.I. Mabuhay! Salamat, Rosey! How do I repay you?

ROSEY:

Just keep us out of the war, General, that's all I ask...that's all I ask. *(laughing)*

You know what? You're the only man I *ever* see eye to eye with.

They both laugh and dance out of the camera range. The camera pans to SOLANGE, a page-boyed brunette in her late 20s with a stunning figure. She wraps herself around an RAF Commander on the dance floor.

SOLANGE:

I know a great spot in the garden where we can go...undetected—so private, Georgie Porgey, *(purring)* alone.

COMMANDER RAZAVET:

Every poor bloke in this room knows your dialogue by now, Solange...all heard the same pitch before. Some, three times. You can only fool the newcomers...not many of them tonight, eh, what?

SOLANGE: *(sensuously rubbing the commander's neck)*

Let's goooo...nooow...now.

Razavet purposefully dances up to PETER PERKINS, standing at the bar.

RAZAVET:

Here you go, Peter, old chap...believe she needs a spot of the old Darjeeling....

A man with a look of one who has done this a

thousand times before, Peter leads Solange down a hallway and out of sight.

CUT TO:

EXTERIOR VERANDA

Shelly Mydans sits on the top steps. She is going over her notes. Something moves behind the chair. Shelly turns and stares into a pair of green eyes.

JEANIE: *(softly)*

I don't know who you are.

SHELLY:

That makes two of us.

JEANIE:

You gonna tattle on me?

SHELLY: *(shaking her head)*

Bet you see a lot from here.

JEANIE:

And hear a lot, too. Everyone's talking about a war tonight. Do you think there's gonna be a war?

SHELLY:

Would you be afraid?

(Pause for a beat. Jeanie cocks her head.)

JEANIE:

I don't know what I'm supposed to be afraid of.

SHELLY: *(Shelly reaches out and strokes Jeanie's hair.)*

And, darling...I hope you never find out.

A cute, middle-aged, typical Yankee-stock couple passes by. Jeanie puts a hand to her mouth to suppress a giggle.

JEANIE:

They didn't see me...that's the Bunnells, Bunny

and Gladys. They're Goodrich Tire maggots, you know.

SHELLY: *(amused)*

I think that's "magnates."

JEANIE:

There's my Uncle Conrad and Auntie Ruth. He bites his fingernails, and she lets me wear her angora sweater, sometimes. Oh, lookie...that's Francisco coming up the steps...he's the High Commissioner's chauffeur. He wears ladies' dresses. *Shelly turns her head, smiles into space.*

CUT TO:

INTERIOR DINING VERANDA

Walter is talking to a group of dinner guests at his table. He puts his hand on the shoulder of ROKAMURA, a middle-aged, erect Japanese gentleman in a constable's dress uniform.

WALTER:

...and Captain Rokamura here has been Chief of Police and family friend for a good many years. He must be doing something right. He and his wife, Seiko, have nine children. *(laughter)*

A bespectacled, proper British emissary rises from his chair and extends a hand to MARIA MARTINEZ, a smart-looking Filipina sitting next to him. She pats her cultivated hairdo as she also rises.

EMISSARY:

I'd rather be dancing with the first woman stock broker on the New York Exchange...*(muttering under his breath)*...enough rapid-fire questions on British security...*(aloud)*...and happily, to be the only man in the world to hold that distinction.

(Maria smiles wryly, recognizing a polite cut-off)

CUT TO:

EXTERIOR VERANDA

George Woods saunters over to the chair where Jeanie is hiding. He squats down into a sitting position on the floor, takes a sip of his drink, and winks at Jeanie. He slowly slides a package and some cookies behind the chair.

GEORGE:

Old George spotted you a long time ago...from Shanghai, kiddo...think you'll like it...befitting a future wife of mine...cookies are a bonus.

Jeanie rips open the package and pulls out an elegant brocade jacket. She quickly puts it on, and reaches over to give George a big hug and kiss.

JEANIE: *(excitedly)*

Thank you, George...I love it. Are you really going to wait for me? Will you?

GEORGE:

I only marry women who get lots of sleep.

He blows her a kiss and starts to rise. Walter walks over, moves the chair slightly, and bends down to pick up Jeanie. The orchestra is playing a waltz. Walter smiles at George and gives Jeanie a kiss.

WALTER:

How 'bout one dance for my girl, before bed?

Jeanie lays her head against Walter's shoulder as he picks her up and waltzes her once around the room, then to her bedroom. The camera pans across the room again.

DISSOLVE TO:

INTERIOR MASTER BEDROOM—NEXT MORNING

Sascha is sitting up in bed finishing breakfast from her bed tray. Walter comes out of the bathroom with a towel wrapped around his waist, walks over to her and bends down to give her a long, lingering kiss.

SASCHA:

Mmmmm...you're better than breakfast...but the kids will be in any moment. Great party! Remember, hmmmm? ...Monday mornings?

After a knock, the door suddenly opens, and the amah comes in with three month old, BUDDY, and three year old, DORIS.

WALTER: *(amused)*

Ah, yes...now I remember! Darl, I ate breakfast with Jeanie before she left for Manila. She got off all right. Damn, she's a trooper!

He rocks the baby who is making gurgling noises.

DISSOLVE TO:

EXTERIOR ARMY JEEP DRIVING ON A ROAD—DAY

An Army jeep careens down a plantation road and rounds a bend, spraying dust into the air. Two soldiers are in the front seat talking excitedly; one is trying to read directions from a piece of paper. A young Filipino boy sits in the back seat, holding on to his hat with one hand, pointing ahead with the other.

BOY:

Here, here. Turn here...they live here!

The jeep turns into the driveway of Walter and Sascha's house, driver waves aside the guard at the gate, almost runs down a surprised gardener and screeches to a stop under the portico. They run up the stairs and start to knock, just as the houseboy opens the door.

CUT TO:

Walter, hearing the commotion, walks hurriedly into the room.

SOLDIER:

Sorry for the intrusion, sir. We're alerting everyone that Honolulu....

DISSOLVE TO:

INTERIOR MASTER BEDROOM

Sascha, having heard part of the commotion, quickly leans over the bed and reaches to turn on the radio. It makes a static, fine-tuning noise.

ANNOUNCER:

...and while Honolulu basked in the early morning quiet, the Japanese maneuvered a sneak-attack bombing on Pearl Harbor... *(static)*...casualties run into the ...*(static)* ...Roosevelt has declared war!

Walter walks hurriedly into the bedroom and throws open the closet door, rummaging for something to wear. He throws some clothes on the bed and sits down. Sascha and Walter stare at each other, listening in horror. Doris is walking in a pair of her mother's high-heeled shoes, oblivious to her surroundings. The baby lies kicking his legs.

Heavy droning of planes can be heard in the distance, gradually getting louder.

DISSOLVE TO:

EXTERIOR MRS. SCHAY'S LARGE HOME IN MANILA

JUAN, the chauffeur, is seen polishing the limo,

which is parked in front of the steps. From inside the house, a woman's voice is heard in loud rhythm, "HUP, HUP, HUP," in cadence with the clap of her hands.

The camera pans to the interior through the window. MRS. SCHAY, a rather severe-looking, dark-haired woman is seen clapping her hands as Jeanie and another little girl are crawling around the room, stretching like cats to the beat. Heavy droning sound of planes gets louder. Mrs. Schay looks upward, worried. The earth shakes as bombs are dropped in the distance. The two girls begin to scream. The house rattles, breaking antique vases and mirrors. The woman lunges for the screaming children and covers them with her body.

CUT TO:

EXTERIOR MRS. SCHAY'S HOME

The amah and Mrs. Schay are running down the steps with Jeanie's leg braces. The chauffeur carries Jeanie to the waiting car.

MRS. SCHAY:

You go right home, Juan. You'll know the safe way. Keep away from the port area. Nichols and Clark may have gotten it, too. Hurry!

CUT TO:

EXTERIOR STREETS OF MANILA

The limo is in traffic. Streets are crowded with cars and caromatas and milling Filipinos, loaded with belongings. Traffic becomes congested. At times, the limo is almost at a stand-still. Bombing in the distance can still be heard. Jeanie stares out of the window in fright. The amah and Juan chatter quickly in Tagalog.

CUT TO:

EXTERIOR JEANIE'S HOME

Sascha runs down the stairs with one of the houseboys, toward the limo coming up the driveway. She opens the back door and grabs Jeanie and hugs her.

JEANIE: *(excitedly)*

Mommy, I was so scared. Mrs. Schay's house was shaking so much...bombs were dropping and fires *(sobbing).* It was scary, Mommy.

SASCHA:

Oh, no...if we had only known, darling! We were damn fools to even think of sending you today. Are you all O.K?

A faint droning of planes can be heard in the distance. Sascha looks up; Jeanie puts her hands over her ears and continues to cry. The droning gets louder. The houseboy grabs Jeanie and they all run into the house.

CUT TO:

A SEQUENCE OF QUICK SCENES:

–Sugar workers running from the fields, getting into carts, pulling water buffaloes out of the water, herding children into ditches.

–Sugar Central operators busy at their switchboards. Sascha and servants packing stuff into boxes, running around measuring windows, and cutting black cloth.

–Jeanie trying to pack her dog, Lady, into a suitcase. Doris walking around in Sascha's high-heeled shoes with black cloth over her head.

–Army soldiers building an airstrip, camouflaging trucks and jeeps.

DISSOLVE TO:

INTERIOR PLANTATION OFFICE

The windows are covered with blackout curtains. Only two dim lights illuminate the office. Walter, his brother, CONRAD, and co-workers are rushing around, pulling files and packing papers. Planes are droning in the distance, getting louder. The mill whistle blows. Walter picks up the ringing phone.

WALTER:

...bombing at Clark Field...Nichols...all the ammo dumps...sure, they're scared! What?...two hundred women and children?!... British?... Here?.... Hell, we'll be ready!

Walter puts down the phone.

Got that, Con? We'll put them in the bowling alley.

CONRAD:

Got it!!...When?

Walter gets up from his desk. He stops short, and picks up a framed photograph of himself and Conrad, their brother Karl, and their father and mother. He stares at it tenderly.

WALTER: *(preoccupied)*

Yah!...in the morning...I'm glad the old man and Mother got out in time. Karl, too. They'll probably worry about us...can't get through to them...keep trying today.

He hands the picture to Conrad. They hug and slap each other's back and walk out.

CUT TO:

EXTERIOR ENTRANCE GATE TO PLANTATION

Army trucks with refugee women and children enter the gates and proceed through the plantation. Planes are heard droning in the distance.

CUT TO:

INTERIOR LIVING ROOM OF CONSTABLE ROKAMURA'S HOUSE

Walter, Conrad, and a U.S. Army Colonel stand in the middle of the room. SEIKO is crying softly, surrounded by her children. The Constable looks straight ahead at his wife and smiles warmly. Walter, looking crest-fallen, hands the hat and swagger stick to Rokamura.

WALTER:

Just a formality, you understand...it means nothing.

CONRAD:

We tried to tell them you are family, but the Army insists...comes from Roosevelt.

ROKAMURA:

Please, don't feel bad. I understand.

Rokamura turns on his heel, erect and proud. He puts on his hat and leads the way out of the door, into the waiting Army car.

CUT TO:

INTERIOR BOWLING ALLEY BAR

A group of dusty young Army men walk into the bowling alley bar and order a round of beers. Walter, Sascha, Conrad, his wife RUTH, and other people cheer at the men.

ARMY MAN #1:

Doesn't look good—we'll try blocking them to the north.

ARMY MAN #2:

Some of the U.S. guys lost their platoons ...

banding with the guerrillas to get a strong task force.

ARMY MAN #3:

Hope to see you folks stateside one of these days...we're out of here, pronto.

CONRAD: *(to bartender)*

Set 'em up, Sixto. One more for the road. Their money's no good here!

CUT TO:

EXTERIOR SWIMMING POOL

Children and mothers are swimming as planes overhead become louder. Bombs drop close by. One of the fathers runs over and herds as many kids as he can to lie down under trees. People are screaming and running. Bombs continue. Planes fly closer to the ground, surveying the damage. Jeanie is seen shivering in a heap of wet kids.

CUT TO:

INTERIOR BREAKFAST ROOM—DAY

The family is having breakfast. The radio announces war news.

SASCHA:

After yesterday's bombing and all the casualties, the women and children left for Manila. Darl, please, let's go.

WALTER:

Go where, for Christ's sake? Tell me. They hit here...Manila ...go where? Stay by the shelters for the time being. When the mill whistle blows, get in fast. I'll try to get the word on our next move. Darl, I'm sorry.

Walter gets up, kisses Sascha quickly, and reaches for his briefcase. She gives him a quizzical, tender look. He kisses her again, passionately.

I have to get to the bank in Manila ...a lot of money to get rid of. I'll be gone all day...trying to get through to the old man in the States...no luck. *He runs out the door.*

CUT TO:

INTERIOR JEANIE'S HOUSE, CHRISTMAS DAY

Jesus, the cook, is carrying a scrawny tree with some Christmas ornaments. He places it beside the dining table where the family is having Christmas dinner. He bows mockingly, waving an arm to present the tree. The family clap with gusto, and all yell "Merry Christmas."

SASCHA:

These are wonderful chicken sandwiches, Jesus, and thank your lovely wife for the lumpia...just delicious. Next year....

Walter rises and toasts to Jesus and all the servants, who have now gathered with small packets of food. He reaches to a side table, picks up some envelopes, and hands one to each of them.

WALTER:

Not very much this year, but thank you for everything. Merry Christmas! You are all so wonderful!

Sounds of planes, getting louder. Everyone glances upward and bolts from the room.

CUT TO:

INTERIOR LARGE TILE BATHROOM

Jeanie's family are all huddled on the floor, bomb

sticks in mouths. Buddy is nursing, Jeanie is sitting in Walter's lap. Doris is on the potty chair, singing. Bombing is heard close by.

JEANIE: *(patting Walter's face, nervously)*

Is it time to be scared yet, Daddy?

CUT TO:

INTERIOR LIVING ROOM OF HOUSE—NIGHT

From the hallway, Jeanie is watching Sascha and Walter, who are standing by the open window, looking at a sky lit from gunfire. Walter has his arm around Sascha. They are talking quietly. Jeanie hugs her dog, Lady, and crawls back to her room.

CUT TO:

INTERIOR JEANIE'S BEDROOM

Walter sits on Jeanie's bed and wakes her gently, calling her name. She wakes up and Walter takes her onto his lap.

WALTER: *(tenderly)*

We have to get to Manila, Jeanie love. We're going to leave while it's still dark. The car is all packed.

JEANIE:

I can take Lady, all right, Daddy?

WALTER:

Only your dolly and some food.

Jeanie starts to cry as Walter dresses her.

CUT TO:

EXTERIOR FRONT OF HOUSE—PRE-DAWN

The servants are checking items in the car. Lady tries to jump into the car, but is pushed out.

JEANIE: *(hugging Lady)*

You stay right here with Ibarra. We'll only be gone for a few days...we'll show those awful Japs...we'll send them back home right away. Then we'll be together again.

Jeanie gives Ibarra a hug and pats Lady lovingly. The rest of the servants are crying. They all hug the family. The family gets into the car, taking Esperanza and Jesus with them. Jeanie and Doris look out the rear window as the car drives away.

DISSOLVE TO:

EXTERIOR COUNTRY ROAD—DAWN

The family car is seen driving on main road, passing a small barrio, void of any activity. People are seen peeking out of closed shutters. A roar of engines is heard, growing louder. The car pulls to the side of the road, under a tree. The camera pans to the interior of the car.

WALTER:

Keep the kids quiet...don't know what's ahead.

Jesus motions for them to duck down. He gets out and pretends to check the tires. The noise gets louder. Trucks of Filipino and American soldiers pass them going south. The family relaxes. Jesus starts the car and drives off.

SASCHA:

I don't like this...gives me the willies. How much longer?

WALTER:

Darl, no use wondering...save your strength... it may be hours.

A heavy drone of engines is heard, getting louder. Jesus pulls the car under a tree by a small Nipa house and a bridge. Walter opens the car door and strains to listen. He jumps out, pulling everyone with him. A man and a boy come out of the house, shooing them away.

WALTER: *(grabbing the baby)*

Stay down! Stay close to the house! Follow me...down on the ground! Crawl, Jeanie!

Jesus shuts the car doors and they follow Walter under the bridge. They lie in muddy water. The sound of the engines gets louder. The family try to keep their heads above the mud. Doris starts to cry. Sascha muffles her with a hand. A male American voice speaks.

VOICE:

Just stay where you are. You're doing fine. We're U.S. soldiers, trying to blow up these bridges before the Nips. Damn! Mitsubishi moon above...stay put!

Walter is holding Jeanie above the muddy water and balancing the baby.

WALTER:

This is your chance to play in the mud, Jeanie, baby. *(He winks at Jeanie.)*

Different engine sounds are heard—lower, closer to the ground, becoming louder. Suddenly, strafing bullets from low aircraft riddle the bridge and the water around them. The strafing continues for another ten minutes.

Agonizing screams are heard in the distance. Sascha's hand is over Doris' mouth, the child is still hysterical. The family huddles. The planes do not return. Jesus takes Doris from Sascha.

SOLDIER'S VOICE:

O.K. folks, get the hell outta here...this one's

next. We'll say hello to Tojo for you...
with one of these.

The soldier comes into view, dirty and wet, holding heavy dynamite over his head. He kisses it and crawls away in the water.

The family makes their way back to the road, crouching behind bushes. They stop at the car, noticing bullet holes on the car roof. Fresh blood drips from a tire. A trail of blood leads to the house. Sascha's half-guttural sob does not go unnoticed. Jeanie's muddy face freezes in terror as she steps over a child's torn arm lying on the ground. Walter spots the bloody arm, grabs Jeanie close, and lifts her into the car. She looks down. There is blood on her legs, braces, and shoes.

JEANIE: *(crying)*

What's that, Daddy? Is it dead? Does it belong to someone?

CUT TO:

EXTERIOR APARTMENT HOUSE IN MANILA—DUSK

BUNNY & GLADYS BUNNELL are seen running down the stairs of the apartment house as the family's car pulls up.

BUNNY:

Oh, no! This is too much...are you hurt? The blood, oh...

GLADYS:

Come dears, quickly...hot baths and whiskey sodas. Bed for the kids. Come, Jesus, leave the car.

Outdoor food preparation area at Santo Tomas.

Jap Plan for Six Invasions of the American Mainland

Here is an English Translation of the Nipponese War Map

THE Japanese map showing six invasion routes to the U. S. is supposed to represent the northern half of the globe. The white spot in the center of the map is the North Pole. At the right edge of the globe is South America and at the far left is Africa. North America and Asia are in the center and the northern part of Australia peeps up from the bottom. The map was originally published on the front cover of a big Japanese picture magazine like Life or Look.

YANK
THE ARMY WEEKLY

From *Yank-The Army Weekly*, April 28, 1944

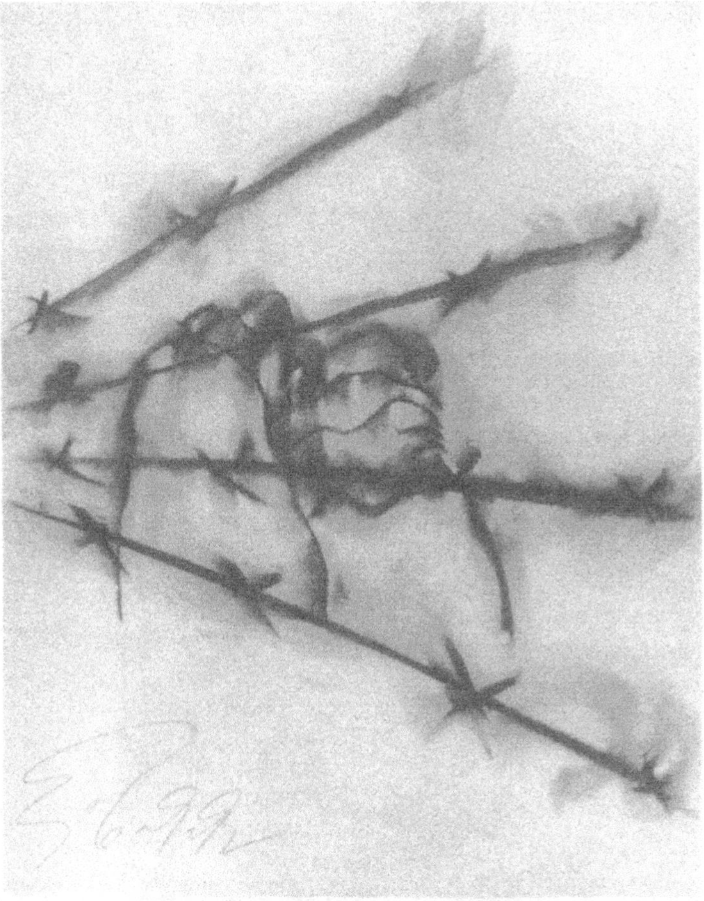

This is What Happens..., #VI, by E.J. Gold,
charcoal on Sennelier Pastel paper, $12^{3}/4$" x 16", 1992.

Sketch of Karen Kerns at Santo Tomas done by Louise K. Cookingham, 1944. Note initials on Karen's hat, "S.T.I.C."

Karen in her art studio, Ojai, California, 1994.

Karen Kerns Lewis

These are the memoirs of Karen Elizabeth Kerns Lewis, interned in the Japanese prison camp of Santo Tomas University in Manila, The Philippine Islands, from January 1942 to February 1945. The rights to her story belong jointly to her and to her daughter, Arden Teresa Lewis-Mount, who is developing a fictional version of her mother's story.

Balatoc, Philippine Islands, 1941 –

The history books are wrong about the date of the bombing of Pearl Harbor. It was on a Monday, not a Sunday, that the Japanese attacked, and it was December 8, 1941. I remember this so clearly because my mother came into my room before dawn, as I was awaking, to say that she was keeping me home from school that morning, having decided that it would not be safe to leave our home in Balatoc and go into Baguio City.

Mother had been up early and had heard the news about Pearl Harbor on the radio. Always right, and a little psychic, she knew immediately that the Japanese bombers would be on their way to the Philippines to destroy the American Army Air Force Base next to my school in Baguio. So that morning I was kept home and did not join my school chums on the bus ride from our mining community to the Brent School in Baguio. I was not with my friends and teachers as they huddled in prayer under the chapel seats when the Japanese bombed Camp John Hay next door. For the moment, I was safe. I was nine years old.

It was perhaps two weeks later that Mother and I found ourselves on a bus heading south to Manila. A nine-year-old's sense of time is uncertain. I do remember that the days following the attack on Pearl Harbor were filled with first aid classes and preparation for war, injury, and starvation. My mother and I learned how to roll cotton onto the ends of little sticks, fold bandages, and pick our way along a narrow foot trail worn into a sheer mountainside that dropped a thousand feet to a rock-strewn river below. This narrow path led to a cave stocked with medicine, food, water, and, of course, our cotton swabs and bandages. We had to practice getting to the cave a lot in order to become sure-footed under a crisis of either Japanese bombing, or invasion, or attack in the dark of night.

It was almost two weeks later when the night crisis did come, but it was in the unexpected form of an order to evacuate the gold-mining community and send all of the women and children to the safety of Manila. It seemed that the Japanese Army had landed on Luzon Island at Linguyen Bay, which was a lot closer to Baguio than to Manila. And we did live at the site of one of the great gold producing mines of the Philippine Islands. So it was time to get out, and that was the one scenario we had overlooked in all our practicing.

We were asked to leave immediately, and with only one suitcase each. My mother took me to the closet to show my hidden Christmas presents, and I chose two to bring with me. They were a small silver comb-and-brush set and tiny framed photographs of my favorite dolls; all were accessories for the beautiful doll house my mother had designed and I was never to see.

Since we were going to Manila, Mother packed an evening gown and her tennis racket. Within an hour, we were on a bus headed south with the other women and children from the Balatoc Mine, fleeing for our lives before the advancing Japanese Army. We honestly thought we would be coming back after Christmas.

Our escape went slowly. There were convoys of buses heading south, trucks and army vehicles heading north, and hordes of people on foot going in both directions. Our passage was interrupted often by sudden stops to take cover from the high-flying bombers or the road-buzzing fighters with bright red-orange spots under their wings. "Fried eggs" is what we named the Japanese symbol of a rising sun and conquest.

At one of our plunges for cover under roadside camouflage netting, we were startled nearly out of our skins by a barrage of return fire from anti-aircraft guns sharing our camouflage! It was definitely going to be safer in Manila.

Manila was filling with refugees from the suburbs and provinces. Mother and I eventually arrived at the apartment of friends and wondered if we would ever see my father again. We did, on Christmas Day after his three-day walk down from Baguio. The men had stayed behind at the mines and refineries, ordered to destroy the mining operation and bury the gold. Having done this, and carrying whatever gold bullion they could, they walked down from the mountains, 100 kilometers to Manila. Led by Igorot guides along their native foot trails and mountain paths, the men were barely able to stay ahead of the Japanese Army advancing along the winding roads. At the edge of the mountains, the Igorots bade them farewell, and left them on their own to cross the plains and rice paddies to Manila. My father never went back to our house again after seeing us off in the middle of the night.

In the twinkling of an eye, we had left behind a life of privilege and possessions, a life filled with parties, clubs and servants. We had been pampered, isolated American colonials abroad. Things were about to change.

Manila was defenseless and was declared an open city. The military forces had been moved to Bataan and Corregidor, and many civilians, including my mother (a crack secretary), volunteered to help close down the military offices and operations in Manila. Meanwhile, we were bombed and strafed as we hid in basement air shelters, rationed food, and wondered what was to become of us.

The bombing finally stopped, and a nerve-wracking silence took its place. Occasionally we would see a bus load of Japanese soldiers traveling the streets in front of the apartment. Afraid to go out, we could only wonder and wait for a knock on the door. It finally came in early January of 1942.

The door-to-door roundup of the Allied civilian population of Manila, now swollen with refugees, had begun. In fact, it was well under way, as we discovered when we joined thousands of others in Rizal Stadium.

Each of us carrying one suitcase, Mother, Dad, I and our friends were processed and sent to Santo Tomas University, a Dominican school turned into an intern-

camp that was to be our home for the next three years and one month.

There was a popular song of the time called "South of the Border," and we sang these words to its tune:

North of España, in Santo Tomas.
That's where we stand in line
for fish so fine
and tea and mush.
We're all in internment,
and that's where we'll stay,
North of España, for many a day.

Our days in Santo Tomas can be divided into two different stories, affected critically by whether the Japanese were winning or losing. The first part is a story about the way a diverse group of people pulled together to overcome adversity and despair and channeled their individual energies into the powerful force of communal effort. This story took place while the Japanese were winning.

The second part of the story is about this same group of people weakened by starvation and neglect, hanging on to their hope, their sense of humor, and their miserable lives as their bodies deteriorated and slipped toward the eventuality of death. This second story took place as the Japanese were losing and continued until the liberation of Santo Tomas.

Santo Tomas University made a perfect internment camp. Although within the Manila city limits, it was north of the Pasig River and away from the downtown area. The entire campus was surrounded by a high wall, and access could easily be controlled through the main gate. There were two large buildings and two smaller ones, filled with classrooms to house the thousands of Allied civilians being rounded up and interned by the Japanese.

Arriving at the university from Rizal Stadium, we drove through the main gate, down a tree-lined double drive and to the large plaza in front of the elegantly baroque Main Building. There in the plaza, we were unloaded under the *porte cochere* and directed to the lobby of the Main Building where we joined the crowd of Manilaites camped out on the lobby floor. Mother scanned the crowd for familiar faces, and spotting friends we squeezed in beside them. Hungry, tired, and thirsty, we awaited the assignment of classrooms, prisoners all.

I remember curling up with my head pillowed in my mother's lap and being urged to sleep. So many people were crowded into that lobby—friends, acquaintances, strangers. Eventually, we were separated from Dad, and Mother and I were given a blanket and assigned to a room. After wrestling with our unfamiliar mosquito netting, we lay down to sleep at last. The weeks of silent waiting had ended, and life in a Japanese prison camp had begun.

The Santo Tomas classrooms were to be home for the next three years, and our education was just beginning. Women, children, and old men occupied the rooms of the main building; the rest of the men and older boys lived in the rooms of the top two floors of the education building. We were separated at night at curfew and reunited the next morning in the breakfast line, after roll call. We actually moved around quite often to different buildings. As more and more people were brought into camp, two smaller annex buildings were converted to sleeping quarters for women with children. I can recall living in six different places during that three-year period.

All of the men with any previous military service record were taken out of camp, ending up near the end of the war sailing to Japan on a Japanese troop ship that was bombed or torpedoed and sunk by Americans.

New people were constantly being brought into camp as the Japanese secured the outlying provinces. To ease the overcrowding, a great number of internees volunteered to leave Santo Tomas in order to establish another internment camp at Los Baños to the south of Manila. The size of the internee population stabilized, and a rather varied and rich camp life evolved amidst the confining daily routine. This was due in great part to a few American and British businessmen and their efforts to impose the rule of the Geneva Conference upon the Japanese establishment running the camp.

As a child, I had no idea what these rules from Geneva were, but they were being constantly invoked. We had an attitude. It was framed by "They can't do this to us!" and "We'll be out next year." And so our elected committee, empowered with attitude and a hunch that the Japanese would be easier to deal with as long as they were winning, made demands on our civilian Japanese commandant.

In no time at all, the incredible pool of human resources from the pre-war Manila population, now contained in Santo Tomas, was pumped into massive communal action to create a daily life and routine that almost seemed normal. It turned out that the Japanese seemed relieved we were solving our own problems.

Health care and sanitation were early priorities. Afraid of the spread of tropical diseases, dysenteries, hepatitis, bedbugs, and even lice, the interned doctors and nurses set up a hospital and passed out the disinfectant and Mercurochrome. Children were set upon the flies, armed with glass jars, waxed paper, and rubber bands. I remember that prizes were awarded to the winning flycatchers, but not being one, I don't know what they were.

Every man, woman, and child went through regularly recurring bedbug inspection, clearing the sleeping quarters of their mattresses and dragging them out into the sunshine of the plaza to search for and destroy the bedbugs while the empty rooms were disinfected. Of course, we got bitten every day and night anyway as we sat in the classroom chairs that lined our hallways. Everyone also kept a vigilant eye on us kids for possible outbreaks of lice.

Sanitation was a top priority. Engineers and plumbers rigged the pipes in the latrines to create cold showers. Toilet paper was rationed immediately, and everyone over the age of twelve had regular bathroom monitor duty. Eating was not allowed in the rooms where we slept, but only in designated communal areas, including the halls overlooking the courtyards. We stood in line to get our breakfast and our dinner from a communal kitchen staffed by internees, and we stood in lines to wash our own tin dishes and cups in communal hot water that had been boiled in cooking vats. I also remember trying to wash my dishes in cold, greasy, soapy water. Anyway, we did everything for ourselves. Everyone had a camp duty, according to their talent or desire, in addition to KP and bathroom monitor.

The talent array was awesome. Except for the Filipino mestizos and a handful of German businessmen and their families, the entire international population of a major Pacific city and its countryside was interned in Santo Tomas—3,000 people and their skills were forged into a communal effort of combined individual contributions—true camp life. All gave of their talents.

There were the talents of doctors, nurses, businessmen and negotiators, ministers, teachers, entertainers, musicians, writers, artists, college professors, gardeners, cooks, engineers, builders, housewives, hobbyists, whores, and opportunists of all sorts. All made their contributions to camp life. Some of those contributions perhaps gave the ministers a bit more to do, and the committee a little more to mediate.

My mother's love of books and her office skills contributed to her job as a camp librarian, and my father, an accountant for Benguet, a mining company, landed a job in the garbage detail! Talents in great demand were those of craftsman and seamstress.

Especially popular were those who could repair shoes and make bakias (a wood-soled flip-flop), who could fashion plates, cups, and water carriers from cans, who could crochet brassieres to fit and knit shirts—all out of string—and who could patch and repair worn-out garments and create a new pair of shorts from old skirts or trousers. Fortunately our weather was tropical, so we went native and lived in shorts and shirt-sleeves. And the most favored talent with the children was that of the clever ladies who could sew from the tiniest of scraps a small stuffed animal to hug.

There most certainly was some sort of barter or payment for these skills. As a child, I knew little of this, but small gifts often were exchanged, and tooth fairies never let us down, even if only to deliver a coveted piece of colored chalk or a purloined macaroon. Most everybody had brought some money and jewelry into camp, and some found ways to smuggle in more money and goods to exchange. I remember using the Japanese-issue money; we called it Mickey Mouse, but it did buy food and cigarettes. I was too young at 10 and 11 to appreciate the wheeling and dealing of grownups that brought a little extra food or a pair of shorts, or a privacy screen or cigarettes—or eventually, an outdoor shanty in a designated family area.

These activities belonged to the adult world. I was a child and the beneficiary. I do remember the sensual delight of allowing a teaspoonful of cocoa honey to melt slowly on my tongue. My father paid dearly for that jar of cocoa honey. Being on the garbage detail gave him the opportunity to participate in some camp smuggling activity.

The price of that particular jar of honey was two

weeks in jail, a small room in the corner of the main lobby. Period. Fortunately, the barred and shuttered window to the front of the building let in some fresh air, the only relief from the heat and stench. Sadly for us, when he was released, he was no longer on garbage detail. Mother and I certainly had enjoyed and benefited from his short life of crime.

Everyone in camp kept very busy with daily chores, both communal and personal: KP, bathroom duty, food preparation, but also teaching, healing, nursing, cleaning. In addition to routinely hauling our mattresses into the sunshine, we were always cleaning and disinfecting our rooms, halls, and bathrooms. We eventually arrived at a tolerable standoff in our fight with the bedbugs, cockroaches, flies, lice, and mosquitoes.

There was free time, too, and plenty of opportunity to fill it. My mother was always improving herself and found time in her busy schedule to perfect her Spanish, express her appreciation of Milton, and annihilate bridge opponents. I think she even played a little Mah Jong. But my poor dad, the former accountant and payroll administrator, began to lose his spirit a little without his rounds of golf, highballs, and cigarettes. The heavy smokers in camp all had a tough time and eventually were reduced to picking up the butts discarded by the Japanese soldiers. I think Dad really missed the excitement of garbage detail.

The loss of dinner parties, golf games, and the other trappings of our previous colonial lifestyle didn't slow everyone down. In the beginning, we still had the energy and determination to establish a kind of summer camp lifestyle unusual in a Japanese prison. Life seemed almost normal to us kids, anyway. And thanks to the talents of a truly dedicated group of teachers also interned from throughout the Manila public and private school systems, we kids went back to school. In no time at all, these amazing people had established grades kindergarten through 12 in an outdoor setting, operating in the shade of the north side of the University's Education Building and underneath the spreading trees.

The classroom chairs removed from our new sleeping quarters were put to good use. Enough textbooks to share or keep on reserve had been rounded up. The math books curiously had been mutilated by blocking out all of the dollar and cent symbols. Instead, we learned in pesos, centavos, kilometers, and kilos, though in camp the Philippine currency had been replaced by the Japanese issue we called Mickey Mouse. This seemed to circulate freely for a while, but eventually we ran out of that, too.

Midway through internment, school classes were moved to the top floor lab rooms of the university's Main Building. This was a definite improvement. We had a roof over our heads and blackboards. I look back with awe and respect for those amazing teachers, so challenged, so inspired, and so brilliant, who, with so little, taught us so much. However, back in the spring of 1942, I could only lament that my unexpected school vacation and journey, which had begun so momentously the previous December, was now ended. I was back in that dread Monday through Friday school-day routine of childhood. But this childhood was going to be different from anything I had experienced before.

Up to the moment of internment, I had been a typical only child, isolated and protected from the world of rowdy kids and rivalry. My friends had been carefully chosen and my playdates and sleepovers thoughtfully arranged to provide maximum social opportunity. My mother had been an only child herself and appreciated the importance of having friends one's own age. And she always made sure I had a pet, usually a cat. She loved cats. I think I would have preferred a dog, but I'm not sure I knew that then. I always did what my mother wanted. I adored her and wished to be just like her. She was my best friend.

Being in Santo Tomas changed all that. I was never again an only child. It was kids' time all day long, from morning roll call through evening curfew to bed-time roll call. It was like being in sleepaway summer camp from age nine to twelve and a half, but having Mom there to tuck you in at night. It was fun! Never mind that we were slowly starving to death, wore rags and lost friends and family members to disease and malnutrition. I was never lonely again.

Loss of dignity, hope, spirit, and health were things for grownups to worry about. Instead, I worried about school, and what old friends were saying behind my back, and whether my new friend wanted to steal my old boyfriend. And I had the pick of every imaginable type of friend: rich, poor, brown, white, American, British, Spanish, mestizo (half Filipino and half any of the above). There even was a smattering of German children whose parents were simpatico to the Allies and who chose internment rather than risk life on the outside in a hostile city occupied by Japanese soldiers.

In fact, many American and British citizens with German names or parentage were given the choice of staying out of Santo Tomas. Eventually they came into camp to avoid the random harassment, life-threatening episodes and rape inflicted by drunken soldiers or resentful natives. It turned out to be safer in camp than outside—but that's a different story.

I went to school and played with every kind of child there was in Manila and its barrios, children of every color, every creed and every background. Parents' social standing mattered little in this new environment. I slept in a classroom crammed wall to wall with cots and mosquito netting, sharing the space with thirty other mothers and children. Privacy and privilege no longer existed. This was ghetto life, and it was chock full of kids my age—of all ages—doing good and bad things to each other all day long. I was surrounded.

Gone from my life were the long rides home from school that divided my days into social exchange and solitude. And gone was the need for my mother to arrange my after-school play dates. For the first time in my life, I was choosing my own friends, making my own plans, even arranging my own after-school dates. I was in prison, but I was truly free.

Not that Mother didn't urge me to choose wisely. I was, after all, only nine years old. Almost ten! And she never gave up on wanting and getting the best she could for me. I was still her one and only child.

One of the earliest privileges she signed me up

for was boarding school. Somehow, in the early part of camp life, a group of parents actually managed to arrange for their children to be enrolled in the Holy Ghost Convent School somewhere else in the city of Manila. So a great number of us were sent away on a bus to experience a better life. There were piano lessons, formidable nuns, burnt eggs, and tripe. I couldn't bear it, and I still associate the scent of Cashmere Bouquet soap with that whole lonely experience.

I just couldn't fit in with any group at Holy Ghost, and I missed the nightly reassurance of my mother's hug and the warmth of her body next to mine under the mosquito netting. I was still an only, lonely child. Miserable in my prison of privilege, I eagerly looked forward to the first visit that the Japanese allowed our mothers. This must have been a high point for the Japanese propaganda machine, because uniformed soldiers with cameras were everywhere, snapping pictures of well-fed, well-educated children and their proud and happy parents.

One of the soldiers followed mother and me around all day. We couldn't shake him, even for me to change into the new red and white floral pinafore Mother had made for me. Finally, after I had put it on and Mother was braiding my hair, he snapped the picture and disappeared. This must have been in July or August 1942. Sailing back to San Francisco after our liberation, in March 1945, Mother befriended one of the wounded, convalescing American soldiers who were returning home with us from their Philippine battles. He made her a gift of a photograph he had taken off a "dead Jap soldier." It was the picture of me in my new pinafore with Mother braiding my hair.

Eventually the Holy Ghost Convent ordeal ended. I think I was able to convince Mother that I was so sad and lonely that I couldn't really eat, play the piano, or study. I begged to return to Santo Tomas and to her.

Finally we were back together, in a brand new room in a brand new building, the Annex, which was for women and children only. I was back in the bosom of big, rowdy family living, making new fast-friends. My mother, who had wangled a spot in the corner of the room, now had twice as much privacy. We were both thrilled. I happily went to fifth grade with my new friends and began to study about Alaska. War? What war?

It seems as if everyone made a point of keeping busy. The ever resourceful grownups of Santo Tomas made sure there was no shortage of enrichment or extracurricular activity, and they marshalled their talents and resources into an amazing menu of education and entertainment for adults and children alike. Sewing ladies taught us to darn and patch. Singers and musicians taught chorus and organized after-dinner group singalongs. Dancers and floor show entertainers taught ballet moves, tap, acrobatics and juggling, and they planned evening entertainments. Linguists taught Chinese or Spanish. Professors taught literature of all kinds.

A lady with red hair in a bun taught me how to recite a James Whitcomb Riley poem before an audience, with feeling and proper inflections ("...And the goblins'll get YOU, if you don't watch out!"). I could have gone to a sketch class with an artist who was doing camp portraits in pastels, and I could have attended, with a group of real serious kids, the reading of *Robinson Crusoe* and other classics by one of their mothers. I was forever being pressured by Mother to be more like that woman's daughter. But I preferred reading to myself fairy tales, myths and *Gone with the Wind*. And to this day, I have yet to read *Robinson Crusoe*.

I had better things to learn in my free time, and I found the best teachers in camp to be other kids! Boys and girls played everything, all together. I perfected my hopscotch, mastered group jump rope and red hot pepper, learned native games like cockfight and keeping a small pompon or paper ball up in the air with my foot. I could throw a knife to carve a wedge from a circle drawn in the mud for a game called Pie, and I could run and jump and feint and dodge in a whole bunch of group games, all the while wearing native wooden bakias, a clog type of sole with a strap across the toe.

I even could climb trees in those bakias, though bare feet were better and safer. We camp kids and teenagers went ape over climbing the beautiful spreading trees that lined the two long drives leading from the gate on España Avenue to the piazza in front of the porticoed entrance to the Main Building.

Climbing those trees was my greatest thrill. We all loved it and got very good at ascending to great heights, inching our bodies out the length of a long limb until our weight would bend the branch to the ground. We would slide off, then climb the tree all over again. This was our most popular pastime, and we became rather territorial over certain trees, all of which were incredible—I wish I knew the names of those trees.

Climbing trees didn't make me a tomboy; my best friends were always the girls. A group of us formed a club with secret nicknames and codes, and we would pester talented teenage girls to draw us glamorous paper dolls, and then spend hours designing their wardrobes.

It really did seem like being in "summer camp." Grownups and children alike called their new home "camp," never "prison." It was Santo Tomas Internment Camp, S.T.I.C. for short. We put those letters on everything—straw hats, cotton shirts, notebooks and diaries. We even wrote it in ink on the backs of our fingers like little tattoos. It was our camp emblem, and it was our badge of courage. We wore it with honor! It went with our attitude. We knew the Allied forces would win eventually and come to save us. We never doubted that for a moment. The big question was when.

At first, we really did believe that we would be liberated very quickly, because the Americans would never let the Japanese get away with keeping us in a prison camp. In the event the war dragged on, we certainly expected to be repatriated. Actually, some of the internees were repatriated though I have no idea how the lucky ones were picked. (Note: "Open City" by Shelly Mydans is her story of the early days of S.T.I.C. and of her subsequent repatriation on the Gripsholm, a neutral Swedish ship.) Their departure helped to feed the fires of hope for the rest of us.

Eventually, we began to notice that the winds of war had changed. CARE packages and exchanges with friends on the outside ceased. Evening entertainments and floorshows stopped. Food rations were reduced. Our civilian commandant was replaced by a general, and groups of soldiers were more noticeable.

I'll never forget the day they began to cut off the limbs of our beloved trees, leaving a few thick, skeletal stubs above the first crotch in each trunk. Tree by tree, the limbs fell along the double rows of the old, majestic canopy of spreading trees that lined the two driveways from the main gate to the piazza in front of the Main Building.

We wanted to cling to the trees, abandoning each in turn before the advancing saws, but we were only allowed to witness the destruction from a safe distance. In a few days, there were no more trees to climb, no more limbs to bend in a slide to the ground—only grotesque shapes of thick trunks abruptly ending in a crown of stubby Y's. I don't think I had ever experienced anything so sad in all my life. But we knew, beyond any doubt, that the Japanese were now losing the war!

There had been clues before this: the loss of little privileges, the tightening of food rations and medical supplies, earlier curfews. But with the increasing presence of the Japanese military, it became obvious to us that the war was not going as well for the Japanese. It also became clear that the earlier cooperation and leniency we had enjoyed had more to do with the Japanese being victorious than with our being outraged or with our camp leaders being eloquent and persuasive.

Angry, indignant, and underprivileged as we were when first thrown into Santo Tomas, those early months of Japanese victory had bought us the time we needed to adapt to having and needing less before facing the challenge of slow, deliberate starvation and true deprivation. That's the second part of my story.

We began to live *on* less and *with* less. We subsisted on a native diet of rice, *camotes* (yams), *talinum* (slippery, healthy green leaves,) and, occasionally, dried fish and soybeans. We dressed in shorts, halters, and shirts and bakias, which were much more appropriate to the humid Manila weather than our sharkskin suits and silk hose and party dresses. We worked all day long at communal chores, slept together in crowded rooms, stood in line for rations and took cold showers. We got tough and tanned and very skinny.

We became strong in spirit and resolve. Even though some internees had a little more than others, as in any community, basically we all had been reduced to the same level. We had developed a strong sense of community—we were all in this together and were all going to make it through. So the second part of my internment story takes place as our bodies, minds, and spirits began to adapt to slow and steady starvation.

One of the strangest activities of camp life, to which we were all addicted, grownup and child alike, was the collecting of recipes. It was not just the collecting of gourmet recipes from world class cooks and famous Manila hostesses (many of whose recipes became the mainstay of Mother's reputation as a post-war hostess), but the acquisition of every recipe that man, woman, or child could get their hands on. Magazines from the late thirties and early forties, with all their mayonnaise, Jello, and meatloaf suggestions, were avidly borrowed and copied. Every recipe that was ever printed or handed down from the previous generation was now eagerly recorded and exchanged again and again. In the back of my math, English, and history notebooks, I collected recipes for carrot casserole and mashed potatoes.

We had gone crazy from hunger and didn't know it. We were like medieval monks in a scriptorium, filling our days with penmanship. As I look back on this obsession, I have to wonder how we ever managed to keep ourselves supplied for so long with ink and paper. Maybe a grownup remembers. I was only twelve, and very hungry. We were consumed by the memories of food as our bodies deteriorated from starvation. Eventually, even copying another recipe became too great a physical and mental activity.

Our food rations had been steadily dwindling, and now we lined up twice a day for a watery gruel. I'm not sure just when we had stopped receiving the occasional Red Cross package or peanut butter, or ration of dried fish.

I do remember, towards the end, holding soybeans in my mouth one by one, savoring them until I could no longer resist the need to chew. Then I would swallow each one as slowly as possible. Soybeans were a rare treat. And even before things got that bad, I remember sucking pebbles and loving their earthy taste and warmth.

The starvation diet started its assault on our bodies. Beriberi and dysenteries were common, as were amoebas and parasites. I don't remember much malaria, but it was there. Spraying the mosquito population of camp was high priority throughout the three years, as was controlling bedbugs, lice, and flies. I don't remember being bitten that much. But we probably didn't taste very good. And at night, we were under mosquito netting and left the hunt to the bats that flew through the open windows of our high-ceilinged rooms.

By the time I was in seventh grade, I had become too weak to climb the stairs to the top floor of the Main Building, where our classes were now being held. Always a good student, I had really enjoyed fifth and sixth grades, but now I could not focus or concentrate on the Spanish lessons or the math.

In looking back on my life, however, I think something else was contributing to my malaise. I was of course weakened by hunger, but I also was twelve years old. My close circle of friends was changing, as were our bodies and our interests. Some were growing breasts, and paper doll dresses were less important now. Out of the blue came a new girl friend into our circle who charmed my pals away.

I was jealous and hurt; I remember feeling very lonely as I climbed the stairs to seventh grade, kind of the way I had felt at the Holy Ghost Convent, my one bout with boarding school. I managed to convince my mother that I was too weak to go to school and, as I hadn't been doing well anyway, she let me withdraw. I never finished seventh grade; I don't think I even completed half of it.

I was tired, weak, and lonely, and I spent a lot of

time in bed. My mother worried constantly about me and stayed near. I liked that. She was still my best friend.

It was getting harder for everyone to keep going. We secretly doubted whether our bodies would make it, but our spirits were fed constantly by rumors. One of the privileges we had enjoyed from the beginning of internment was the PA system that the Japanese had set up for camp announcements, roll calls, reveilles, and curfews.

Our regular camp announcer, a former Manila broadcaster name Don Bell, was quite a wit. He had access to a collection of popular records from which he played songs to wake us in the morning and send us to bed at night. In fact, one of our lost privileges was sitting on our folding chairs in the Plaza to hear nightly concerts from the record collection. Every now and then our clever DJ would use a particular song title or colloquial expression to confirm or allude to the latest rumors or gossip. On the morning after an evening when a new rumor had been circulating, we could expect to be awakened with the song "Rumors are flying, and there's no denying..." All of this would fly over the heads of the Japanese, and we would have another good laugh at their expense and take heart for another few days.

Then one day a new sound drew our eyes skyward; it was a steady droning unlike the sound of the Japanese fighters we were used to seeing. We scanned the skies for its source. Shouts and cries burst from our throats as the tiny speck was located. It was a bomber! Ours! The end of our trial was in sight—we'd be out soon.

Don Bell played "Pennies From Heaven" the

next morning. But no other planes came. Nothing else happened for the longest time, except that the Japanese soldiers got very busy. They built a number of bunkers at the Main Gate and at the entrances to the plaza from the two long driveways. Curfew was moved up, blackouts were begun and we never were to be caught outside looking up at the skies, and our food supplies were cut drastically. Obviously, feeding us was not a priority.

Eventually, there was another episode in the sky. Two fighter planes were in a dogfight. We risked watching this time, with our hearts in our throats. One plane went down in a trail of smoke, and we couldn't see whether its wings sported the insignia of stars or of fried eggs.

We prayed and we waited. This was the worst we had experienced so far, the waiting and the starvation. Our bodies were so malnourished from only two portions of watery rice gruel a day that there was real doubt we could hold on till we were liberated.

As I said, it was those rumors that kept us going. There was no more activity in the sky—we just kept praying and waiting. One day, we heard that MacArthur had landed at Leyte. This rumor wouldn't go away, and the next morning over the PA we were admonished to "get up, get out of bed," and hurry: "Better Leyte than never." As if on cue, the whole camp erupted in laughter.

There wasn't much to do anymore at night, what with the sunset curfew, blackouts and hunger pains, so just about everyone, so weak and tired, went to bed early. Anyway, everybody in our room, which was on the second floor front of the Main Building, had retired early as usual that evening of February 3 in 1945. It had been very quiet; we even had noticed the lack of Japanese soldiers around.

About nine o'clock, there was a terrible clatter and some kind of noise down by the Main Gate. Probably something the Japanese were doing there, which could explain why we hadn't seen them around all evening. But the noise grew slowly louder, sounding like a motor approaching, but rather loud and rumbling, and very hesitant. In no time, everyone who lived on the front side of our building was hanging out their second and third floor windows, curious about the commotion.

The rumbling sound would start and then stop, each time getting a little closer. Our eyes strained to pierce the darkness. Finally we saw that the slowly moving noise was accompanied by an oscillating beam of light that swept back and forth across the pavement before it. As it progressed, the light beam would catch and illuminate the grotesque shape of a truncated tree, first on one side of the drive and then on the other. We watched spellbound as this apparition of noise and light inched its way down the long drive toward us, pausing and creeping.

As it got closer to us, a glimpse of its large armored shape got caught in its waving light, and with one voice we cried out, "It's a tank!" In that very next second, we knew it was ours and that at last the Americans had come to save us.

We yelled and screamed, "There are no mines! It's okay, come on, come on!" Eventually, with our help and encouragement, the tank arrived in the plaza, followed by others of the First Cavalry Division of the United States Army.

At this point, everyone poured out of the Main Building, yelling joyously, to hug and kiss with abandon the emerging G.I. Joes. They were all so tan and healthy, though I remember thinking they were a bit yellow (those quinine pills they took for malaria). We were so thrilled and excited to be liberated that we didn't notice the horror and concern in the soldiers' eyes as they beheld us—emaciated beyond their belief. We looked like human skeletons to them, covered as we were with only our skin and rags.

We didn't see it. We were too high, flying on empty that night. My mother and I were among the first to rush out of the building to welcome our saviors, and the first person Mother ran into was an old friend and bridge partner from her Manila days, *Time-Life* correspondent Carl Mydans, whose wife Shelly had been repatriated earlier from Santo Tomas. He had been caught stateside at the outbreak of the war and had been covering its progress ever since.

The war was far from over, however, and we were not as liberated as we thought. The soldiers were very concerned about the lack of Japanese resistance as they entered Santo Tomas, and questioned us as to their whereabouts. We suddenly sobered as we remembered something we had overlooked in our joy—the absent Japanese soldiers.

It turned out that they were holed up in their offices on the first floor of the adjacent Education Building, with the two floors above them filled with internee hostages: the camp men and boys, our fathers, sons, and husbands, and my dad. We were all herded back into our building, pleading with the Americans not to harm any of our boys and fathers, not to shoot!

We leaned out our windows, our yelling and screaming now frozen in our throats, to watch the tanks line up in front of the Ed Building to open fire against the Japanese and flush them out. The Japanese fired back. My father and most of the other men and boys lived through that frightening experience to tell their stories of dodging ricocheting bullets, hiding for cover and attempting escape.

For the most part, the Japanese soldiers did not use the internees as human shields, but they did come up to their two floors in order to shoot down on the tanks, so my father and everyone else got caught in the crossfire. In their panic, a number of the men, forgetting how weak and frail they were, attempted to escape by lowering themselves down the back of the building on knotted sheets. Tragically, they were too weak to hold on and fell to their deaths within the very hour of liberation.

Fortunately for us, my father avoided this untimely salvation, choosing instead to watch and duck the bullets. After it was over and the Japanese had surrendered, he told us how one soldier rushed into the room, pushed Dad down and ordered everyone to take cover as he positioned himself inside the window and began firing on the Americans. The Japanese resistance was halfhearted, and soon the Americans had routed them all from their strongholds in the Ed Building and from their bunkers.

With their prisoners contained, this advance column of the United States Army now held one prison camp on the northeast outskirts of Manila. Well, actually two prison camps. They were also liberating the internees at Bilibid Prison nearby. It seems that the American Army Intelligence had learned that all the able-bodied Manila prisoners of war were to be sent to work camps in Japan, and the rest—the infirm, the aged, and the very young—were to be killed.

Acting on that information, the First Cavalry Division had pushed ahead of their supporting infantry and supply lines into Manila to liberate the two internment camps.

Though they had brought enough food rations and medical supplies to stay until the rest of the army could catch up, they had no idea how malnourished and weakened we were. They generously shared their rations of beans and chocolate with us. We made pigs of ourselves, our shrunken stomachs and bowels rebelled, and diarrhea was rampant.

The soldiers were wonderful. They shared everything with us—their powdered milk with the children and their coffee and cigarettes with the adults. And we all got such a kick out of seeing these big young men doff their helmets and turn them into cooking pots that fit over their cans of fire. They could warm up wonderful meals from Army rations, or bowls of water for washing or shaving.

As we all waited for the rest of the Army to catch up, there seemed to be little threat from the Japanese, who held the entire city of Manila and all of Manila Bay.

Mother and I were even allowed to go over to Bilibid for a visit with our old Baguio friends, who had been brought down *en masse* by the Japanese sometime after their occupation of Manila and after our incarceration. Bilibid was very different from the sprawling space and loft buildings of Santo Tomas University. It had been an ancient Spanish prison and so was much more claustrophobic, with its open areas confined to walled-in courtyards. But now our years of confinement were behind us, and we were free and happy.

MacArthur himself paid us a visit in Santo Tomas and stood above a large American flag that hung from the portico of the main entrance to the ground below. To this day, I wonder how he got there so fast. Maybe he arrived with the Army. But there he was, congratulating us, the ex-P.O.W.s, for hanging on till he returned, and the First Cavalry for doing such a splendid job of liberating us. Almost dwarfed between the gigantic American flag and the lofty Santo Tomas tower above, MacArthur saluted the crowd and the plaza below with a victory sign and made the cover of *Life Magazine*.

Months later, I scanned that cover's photograph again and again, trying to find my face in the crowd, but I couldn't remember whether I had been hanging out of one of the windows behind MacArthur, or if I was down in the plaza below. It doesn't surprise me that I can't remember this detail when I think of the dramatic events that followed on the heels of MacArthur's departure from the camp.

Within the hour, the Japanese began the shelling of Santo Tomas University, and their first shell hit the plaza. It was just after lunch, the beginning of siesta, on a sunny, bright February afternoon. The plaza was empty except for a few soldiers on the edges seeking shade, and a few kids panhandling the soldiers for chocolate. Not one for taking a siesta, I was looking down on the soldiers from our second story window. Recognizing a pair of twin sisters I knew slightly (they were a year younger than I, which is a lot when you are twelve), I was torn between joining them for a candy bar and delivering a message to a friend on the third floor.

I chose to go to the third floor and idly searched for my friend, circling the whole top floor beginning with the hall on the east side of the building, moving back to the north side and then around to the west hall, finally finding her in the southwest corner room. Looking out one of her windows to the plaza on the south and front of the building, I could see that the twins were still talking to the soldiers and decided to join them.

I had just left the room and was back in the hall, heading for the main staircase, when a horrendous explosion in the plaza rocked the building, tossing me to my knees. It was as if a gigantic thunderbolt had struck the tower or something, and I rushed back into the room to look out the window. A whitish dust was just settling over the plaza, softening the brilliance of the afternoon sun, and through it I could see the bodies of the twins and the soldiers.

I ran from the room and into the hall and toward the stairs to the second floor. There were more explosions, and I think one hit the southwest corner of our building. In my panic, I somehow reached our room and my mother. The Japanese finally had gotten a bead on Santo Tomas University. They may even have been trying to hit MacArthur. They came close! The Army quickly hustled out to the northeast side of the building, away from the shelling which seemed to be falling a little short, mainly hitting the West side of the campus. This was where the gymnasium was, and it took some direct hits.

Sadly, some of the men housed there were killed before the Army could evacuate them. It's hard to reflect on how so many who made it through three years of concentration camp lost their lives or were seriously injured in these first hours of freedom. Obviously the war wasn't over yet.

The fight for Manila was just beginning, and we were the first target. The evacuees from the gym, annexes, and other outlying buildings joined us at our northeast corner, and we all camped out under the stars, reassured by the whistling whine of crossfire as the Americans, their rockets set up behind us, got a bead on the Japanese. We honestly believed that the "Japs" were not capable of lobbing their shells over the building, so, as the Americans were in charge now, we felt safe. But we prayed, for good measure.

My mother, a life-long Episcopalian, had been praying very hard for three years and one month now, using her pretty Roman Catholic rosary that was a gift from a very special nun we had known in Manila. Mother was inconsolable when she discovered she had lost it. Finding it was something we had to do, or die. She remembered last having it in "The Fathers' Garden," a tiny hedged park that ran the length of the building on its western side. This beautiful little garden and grotto had been a place of prayer and meditation for the university faculty and seminarians before the war and, oddly, the Japanese left it alone.

For the internees, too, it became a special place for prayers, solitude, and privacy. I suspect it also was a popular meeting place for midnight trysts. When there was a lull in the shelling—which was often as the Japanese kept moving their mortars to new positions—Mother and I set off for the "The Fathers' Garden" on the vulnerable west side of the building. We never gave a thought to fear or danger and (ever psychic and always right) my mother found her rosary. We returned to the safety of our northern corner in time for the next round of shelling.

This was pretty exciting stuff to a twelve-year-old, and a great adventure. We had all become a little numbed to danger and to death, and we found humor in the oddest things, particularly our bathroom situation. Adjusting as we were to our new diet that was heavy on beans and chocolate, the camp population inflicted some pretty heavy usage on the only two bathrooms available. They were the first floor bathrooms located on the two sides of the building away from the shelling. We stood in long lines as we waited to climb in and out of the first-floor windows to relieve ourselves.

Somehow we joked and laughed that it had all come down to this, confident that it couldn't get any worse. But it did. Those incapable Japanese hit our main waterline. We couldn't run water or flush the toilets.

What had been a laughable inconvenience now had turned into a stinking, disgusting, disease-threatening situation. Again, the Army rescued us. They tapped an outside source for water and soon established bucket brigades to bring it to the stinking bathrooms. We could now bucket flush after every fourth person. Within hours of this solution, the soldiers began digging us some nice new "army" latrines, and everything was under control by the end of the next day.

At least I think it was the next day. At my age then, I did not focus on exact times, or dates, or the lengths of the situations that were momentously unfolding before a backdrop of World War II. I have no sense of sequence for the events that soon led to my mother, father, and I boarding a cargo plane on a back road runway and taking off for the island of Leyte. The rest of the Army, with plenty of supplies, did catch up and join us; the Americans did finally knock out the sources of enemy shelling. Shortwave communication with relatives in the states was established, and the process of sending American ex-P.O.W.s back home was begun.

During this time, many lifetime G.I. Joe-internee friendships were forged. The internees were captured by the kindness and generosity of the G.I.s, and the lonely G.I.s found release from their loneliness with all the American moms and pops, kid sisters and brothers, and even girl friends to fuss over them 9,000 miles from home. One friend of mine ended up marrying her family's adopted G.I. ten years later. My mother kept up a correspondence with two or three of the soldiers until she could no longer lift a pen or think of a thing to say.

But back in late February, 1945, she just wanted to get home—not to Baguio, not to Manila, not even to Los Angeles, but to Montana. My father's parents there both had died while we were in camp, but hers were still alive and well and were living in Stephensville, Montana. So she wangled and she fussed, and somehow we were picked in the first lottery to determine who would be sent home on the first boat. But the Japs still held the city of Manila, Manila Bay, and all the land around except for Santo Tomas, Bilibid, and the northwest province. Thus, all ships set sail for the states from the island of Leyte, where all the American bases were.

So first we had to fly to Leyte, but the Japanese also held all of the airports and air force bases around the city. Getting out of Manila in February, 1945, was not an easy thing to do, and many volunteered to stay behind until they could steam out of Manila Bay! But my mother was determined, and when the announcement came that the first planeload of internees would be taking off that afternoon on a makeshift back road runway north of the camp, my mother and her husband and twelve year old daughter were first in line for the bus.

My last memory of Santo Tomas was being just outside the large entrance to the Main Building in the plaza, waiting to board the bus. It was a sunny late afternoon, but the sun was still high enough for me to see the bright orange glow of burning fires, which defined the western horizon. I could hear a distant thunder of cannon and gun fire.

The battle for possession of Manila was raging, but the broadcaster to my right was sending confident reassurances stateside over his wireless. He was telling the folks back home about how on this great day, as the first group of liberated internees were beginning their journey home to the states, the American forces were at the same time successfully retaking the city of Manila and that it was just a matter of some mopping up and it would be all over. But everyone in the plaza knew that the Battle of Manila had just begun.

Mother and I waved goodbye to some of the best friends we would ever have, and we set out for the plane that waited for us on a back country road now appropriated by the Army Air Force for their landing strip. We piled in and made ourselves as comfortable as possible for the long trip to Leyte. Actually, comfort was out of the question as we were each in a metal bucket seat without the cushioning of a parachute or any fanny flesh of our own. But we didn't care; it was the first flight to freedom and my very first ride in an airplane ever!

You can imagine our dismay when the plane hit a pothole as it was taxiing and broke something, causing us to lurch and come to a stop. We all had to get off the plane and were almost sent back to camp. But a smaller plane was available for the trip to Leyte on the condition that some people would volunteer to stay behind. Pleading and begging and being adamant worked again, and my mother secured a place for us on the smaller plane.

Just after sunset we were airborne and on our way to Leyte. The war wasn't over, but we were free. Our minds and bodies and spirits had been tested almost beyond endurance, but we had all survived, and we had changed in the process.

I had been a shy, protected nine-year-old, an only child in an isolated mining community that was an outpost of American colonialism. Now I was twelve and a half and had just completed three years of tough training camp: Santo Tomas Internment Camp, S.T.I.C. I had experienced the rough and tumble of ghetto living, the sharing and love of communal life, and the toughening of body, and of spirit and resolve, that starvation and poverty can sometimes provide. I had learned to live in a fishbowl and respect the code of privacy. And I had learned most effectively that life provides exciting adventures, and that good always wins in the end.

Weeks later, as we were sailing into San Francisco Bay, my parents believed that their greatest trial was behind them. I believed that mine was yet to come—that of adapting to a society of American teenagers. My training had been good. I was ready.

View of Santo Tomas Internment Camp, 1945

"Gigi" Poston's watercolor sketch of Santo Tomas shanty.

800 Arrive Here on Ship Of Freedom

The largest group of freed Americans—more than 800—to arrive here after three years of hunger in Japanese prison camps and a life in the wilderness of the Philippine jungles, docked yesterday.

After the blood-thinning tropical heat of Los Banos, Santo Tomas and Bilibid, the arrivals, mostly civilians, all wore khaki uniforms and wrinkled Army overcoats to shield them against the rain and cool wind.

Below decks in the transport, before the "Go Ashore" signal had been broadcast, scores of children and babies sat on their tiered bunks waiting to see a country many of them had only heard about.

ALL GET RATION BOOKS

All the civilians began their new life with ration books in hands—puzzling books with airplane and tank coupons, and red and blue stamps that said "2" on them even though they were worth "10."

There were scores of Catholic priests and Protestant missionaries aboard and 45 merchant seamen. There were laborers, druggists, accountants, engineers and miners.

And there were women whose husbands had been taken off to prisons in Japan.

The many-decked transport was a jumble of children and baggage. Many families had their luggage packed in rattan hampers.

CROWD LINES DOCK

And the largest number of relatives and friends ever to greet returning prisoners lined the picket fences on the dock.

One mother, waiting below decks with her children in the great Coast Guard transport, turned on the tap water in a stateroom and was delighted to find the water came out cold.

Others hurried their children onto

Continued from Page 1

the deck because the Red Cross had tables loaded with coats and sweaters for the shivering youngsters.

A Spanish Dominican priest, The Reverend Father Pelegrin de la Puente, was welcomed by the pastor of Old St. Mary's Church here, Father Thomas F. Burke. Father de la Puente wore a U. S. Army jacket over his cassock and he told how he had been imprisoned at Santo Tomas University, where he had taught before the war.

Another civilian, 28-year-old George Brown of Washington, D. C., was greeted by a one-time fellow prisoner of the Japs, Mrs. L. B. Jepson of Vancouver, B. C.

Mrs. Jepson, whose husband was the Manila agent for the American President Lines, had known Brown in Santo Tomas before she and her daughter, Margaret Ann, were repatriated. Jepson has remained in the Philippines.

The ship's newspaper was edited with the assistance of a New York Times correspondent, H. Ford Wilkins, who was also city editor of the Manila Daily Bulletin before Manila's downfall.

"The town's a wreck," he told reporters. "There are only two rotary presses left in Manila and they are damaged. But Roy Bennett, publisher of the Bulletin, has stayed behind to try and get the paper out again."

Wilkins said he worked on a prison camp newspaper in Santo Tomas but the Japs didn't like it. So for nearly two years the camp had no news sheet.

"For a while," he said, "the Japs allowed the Manila Tribune, which they'd taken over, to be distributed in the camp. But when the war news got so bad that their own propagandists couldn't cover it up, even that paper was discontinued."

And the only Merchant Marine cadet-midshipman held captive by the Japs came home to his parents in San Francisco. He is William T. Mitchell of 111 Santa Ynes avenue, whose father, William Mitchell, is a member of the San Francisco Fire Department. The father was a prisoner of the Germans in the last war.

Article from the Oakland Tribune, April 9, 1945

Oakland Tribune

EXCLUSIVE ASSOCIATED PRESS . . . WIREPHOTO . . . WIDE WORLD . . . UNITED PRESS

VOL. CXLII — OAKLAND, CALIFORNIA, MONDAY, APRIL 9, 1945 — 13 C — NO. 99

HOME—AT LAST—TO 'LAND OF LIBERTY'

David Nuffaly, home from Santo Tomas, kisses his daughter-in-law, Mrs. Lester Nuffaly of Oakland.

Tonya Tupin, 6, showing here how well she can write her name, was "queen of the ship" that brought the returnees.

Louis Mee, 45, didn't have to voice his happiness in "English." A merchant seaman, he was just happy to be back and that's what he said: "Happy."

James Tulloch, of Berkeley, chucks the chin of his baby son, William, born four months ago in the Japanese prison camp at Santo Tomas. Mother, Jean, looks on with a proud grin.

A guerilla leader for 18 months, Garret Mosse (left) finally was captured by the Japanese. He was beaten for two months, then nursed back to health by Carl Gete, Filipino-American youth who returned with him.—Tribune photos.

Front page from the Oakland Tribune, April 9, 1945

Reader Notes

Reader Notes